The Bo
for the Loins

paul scanlon

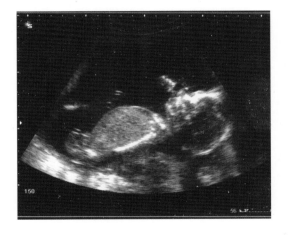

'YOUR EYES SAW MY UNFORMED BODY.
ALL THE DAYS ORDAINED FOR ME
WERE WRITTEN IN YOUR BOOK
BEFORE ONE OF THEM CAME TO BE.'

PSALM 139.16

abundant life publishing

Abundant Life Publishing
Wapping Road, Bradford
West Yorkshire BD3 0EQ

First Published in 2004

Printed by:
Interprint Creative Solutions
Market Flat Lane, Knaresborough
North Yorkshire HG5 9JA

www.interprint-ltd.co.uk

British Library Cataloguing in Publication Data
A catalogue record for this book is available from the British library

ISBN 0-9538516-1-3

Dedication

I dedicate this book to my darling wife Glenda, the bride of my youth and love of my life. Together for over thirty years, we have raised our four beautiful girls who have now become a secure bridge between us and all still in their loins.

To know Glenda is to love her and to know Glenda's God is to love him. Glenda, you have made God irresistible to our children, I've seen it and watched it for over three decades. Your faith is uncomplicated, strong, deep and totally real, and so is theirs. You have shown our girls what a real woman of God looks like. What better gift could a mother give to her children?

People always mistake you as their sister, not only because you look so young but because you have been like a sister to them. You have been their friend and companion. And you are still the greatest shopper of them all!

In April 2003 we were both present at the birth of our third generation, the unbelievably beautiful Hope Cherish. As our second generation held the third, and then passed her back across the bridge to the first, it was a perfect moment of generational continuity: the loins of origin, the bridge of continuity and the 'Hope' of permanence.

I love you Glenda.

Paul

'A WIFE OF NOBLE CHARACTER WHO CAN FIND? SHE IS WORTH FAR MORE THAN RUBIES HER HUSBAND HAS FULL CONFIDENCE IN HER AND LACKS NOTHING OF VALUE'

PROVERBS 31.10

contents

introduction

This book is the product of many things but three in particular:

- My personal journey in life as a first generation believer, a parent and a pastor.
- My observation of the reinvention and resultant rapid growth of The Abundant Life Church, Bradford, which I have the joy of leading.
- The discovery of a timeless biblical truth, which I had not seen this clearly before, that has transformed the way we reach our city as a Church.

I believe that the truths explored in this book are very significant for the whole Church today. They represent a new way of thinking for many of us and as such will demand some soul searching. However, your efforts will be richly rewarded because you will, maybe for the first time, begin to understand how God sees your life, the lives of those you are reaching, and those yet to be born through them.

The development of thought throughout this book is continuous but the material is presented to you in three sections. Each section is described as a battle and the reasons for this will quickly become apparent as we explore these truths together. The three battles relate to three generations of believers. First generation Christians must fight and win the *Battle for the Loins*, second generation Christians are faced with the *Battle for the Bridge*, and the *Battle for Permanence* is the distinct province of third generation believers.

These distinctions should in no way cause the reader to think that they need only read the section that applies to them! The truth is that whichever generation of believers you personally represent, you must be aware of and understand the conflicts being fought by your fellow Christians in each and every generation. You may even be a fifth, sixth or seventh generation believer and therefore feel that this book has little or no relevance to you. You would be wrong, very wrong! So please read on. I am convinced that within these pages you will find yourself, whatever generation you think you are from, because these timeless truths of God's Word are shaping the success or failure of each successive generation of Christians and will continue to do so until the end.

Here is wisdom for every-day Christian living that will equip us to establish the Church in this generation and ensure, as far as we are able, that our children and children's children continue in the same work, going from strength to strength without any generation halting the momentum... until Christ returns!

Paul Scanlon

1975

The first generation's battle:

The battle
for the LOINS

CHAPTER 1

The Battle for the Loins

This book is about a battle. A battle which the Church must win if we are to see our cities reached for Christ, our nations turning to God and the Church suitably prepared for Christ's return. It is not a conventional battle between two opposing armies fighting over the control of a particular geographical area but a battle for the hearts and lives of people. And more particularly, it is a battle for the lives of the unborn descendants of those people, their children, grandchildren and great grandchildren. This battle will change the face of our world like no other conflict known to humanity. This battle I have come to describe as *'The Battle for the Loins'*.

'Loins' is a little used word in modern English language, so let me explain how God brought it to my attention and has reintroduced it into the language of my church and ministry.

Two priesthoods

In Genesis chapter fourteen we read about Abraham's meeting with Melchizedek, the '*priest of God Most High*' following his defeat of certain kings who had tried to plunder his family and possessions.[1] Melchizedek blessed Abraham and in response Abraham gave Melchizedek '*a tenth of everything.*' The priesthood of Melchizedek therefore predates and existed many years before the tribe of the Levites were appointed to serve the priestly family of Aaron, as well as the spiritual needs of the whole nation of Israel. Collectively they became known as the Levitical priesthood.[2]

The writer of Hebrews takes up the important distinction between these two priesthoods as part of his argument to convince Hebrew Christians that Jesus has an enduring priesthood, similar to that of Melchizedek, which is far superior to the Levitical one which had ended with the close of the Old Covenant era.[3] Part of his argument is that the '*lesser person is blessed by the greater*' which is what happened when Melchizedek blessed Abraham because, '*Levi was still in the body of his ancestor.*' So, Levi in effect tithed to Melchizedek too; the lesser priesthood tithed to the greater one, even though Levi would not actually be born for nearly another hundred years. Levi was involved and implicated in the actions of his great grandfather even though he had not been born; he was '*still in his body*' or as some translations say '*he was still in the **loins** of his father when Melchizedek met him*'.[4]

So, even though Levi was nearly a hundred years down stream of Abraham chronologically speaking, as far as God was concerned the actions of Abraham had a direct effect on his unborn offspring. He was in his loins. The word 'loins' (Greek: ὀσφῦς) as used in this passage refers to 'the seat of generative power.'[5] It is 'a means of describing the solidarity of offspring with their ancestors and their involvement in his actions.'[6] Therefore, when Abraham tithed, all his descendants did too!

generational thinking

This represents a whole new way of thinking for most of us. That's because western societies do not automatically think in genealogies or generations like God does. Our attitude to life is characterised more by maxims such as 'seize the day!' We tend to think just about ourselves, we 'take care of number one' and concentrate only on the things we can do in our lifetime rather than giving much thought to those who will come after us.

This thinking pervades the church too. Some are so sure that Jesus is going to return in their lifetime that they see no need to be thinking about the next generation. 'We are the final generation' they triumphantly inform you, 'so why waste time thinking about the next?' There is no Bible proof whatsoever that any generation can make such a claim, yet we have millions of Christians across the world who are not reaching out or making a difference in society because they've already 'checked out'. In their minds they have already bailed out and are just waiting for the rapture to come and take them out of this troubled world. So while the world goes to hell, they await their heavenly glory.

This is not my concept of church and I don't believe that it is God's either. We are called to be 'salt and light'. We are commissioned to reach our generation and every future one that is born through them. This means we are here for the long haul, we are not going anywhere in the short term and are committed to living and planning for permanence.

the line of faith

The writer of Hebrews, who had a Jewish world-view, understood God's perspective of each successive generation. He understood that what Abraham did would affect Levi because he was *'in the loins of his father'*. Abraham was not, of course, the actual father of Levi, he was his great grandfather. But that is not the point; it is the fact that he was his spiritual father that really mattered. The writer is using the term 'loins' in the spiritual fathering sense and Abraham was credited as being the father of his great grandson because God thinks and works in spiritual generations.

In fact, Levi and everybody after him right up to and including us today, thousands of generations later, can all call Abraham their father if they share the same faith in God that he exercised. Every Christian belongs to the line of faith from Abraham. Paul taught that, '*He is the father of all who believe, in order that righteousness might be credited to them.*' All who walk in his '*footsteps of faith*' are named amongst his children.[7] Therefore, '*those who have faith are blessed along with Abraham, the man of faith.*'[8] Notice he says you are blessed '*along with*' Abraham. How can that be? Because you were in his loins too when he first believed! So, what Abraham did in his life, not just on the day he met Melchizedek, implicated us, set a precedent for us, and has become educational, inspirational and revelatory to us. This includes everybody that has come from the 'loins' of the faith line of Abraham.

Many of the first Christians were Jews, the natural descendents of Abraham, and as such struggled to understand how non-Jewish people could ever be considered to be Abraham's children. However the Apostles spell the issue out clearly. It has nothing to do with their nationality. The true, spiritual children of Abraham are those who share his faith not his blood-line: '*For not all who are descended from Israel are Israel. Nor because they are his descendants are they all Abraham's children. On the contrary, "It is through Isaac that your offspring will be reckoned." In other words, it is not the natural children who are God's children, but it is the children of the promise who are regarded as Abraham's offspring.*'[9] The truth is that Abraham was not a Jew. There was no such thing as a Jew or the Hebrew race when God met Abraham. So, Paul is saying that coming from Abraham's natural line doesn't give you any extra credit with God, neither does it qualify you to call yourself one of Abraham's children: '*Understand, then, that those who believe are children of Abraham.*'[10]

The only people who will enter heaven and be classed as Abraham's children are those who have received Christ by faith, the faith of Abraham. All those people were in his 'loins' when he believed God and from God's perspective, were included in the countless 'stars in the sky' and 'grains of sand on the seashore' that God told Abraham represented his future offspring.

people in the loins

This understanding that God counts past and future generations in one continuous line of faith, has transformed the way we do outreach here at the Abundant Life Church. We have realised that when we reach one lost person, dormant within their loins are their children, grandchildren and every future generation that springs from that new line of faith. We are now thinking beyond the limits of our time-space world and learning to live in the light of God's eternal purpose, which extends far beyond our natural ability to see or comprehend.

In a time-space world you have to wait for things to develop. But God isn't waiting for anything to develop. God is immune from process. He isn't waiting to see what happens, hoping it comes out alright. God effortlessly sees everything that has ever happened and everything that ever will happen. He already sees every child that is in every person's loins, right now. God knows who is going to be born, when they'll be born, what their name will be, what they will do, what kind of life they'll live, and so on. God knew you and saw you before you were born. He was not surprised when you showed up! Your parents might have been but God wasn't, because he doesn't just think about the current generation but about the people *inside* the people who are alive at any point in history.

I believe we need to begin thinking more creatively and deliberately about the 'people inside the people' we are reaching in our towns and cities. That's because the 'people inside the people' we are reaching today are implicated in everything we do for that person, and in that person's response to our initiative of reaching out to them.

We don't tend to think this way because we don't think in generational terms. Many people live just for today. Some live just for their next big event and don't see beyond it. We need to get out of this selfish, short-sighted cultural tendency of not thinking beyond our noses, beyond our next vacation, beyond our next nice outfit, our next hairdo, and next Christmas! We have to start thinking generationally, so that when we look at people we're not just seeing them, we are seeing the 'people inside the people', the people in their loins.

All of us, to some extent, can describe how the things our fathers or forefathers did affected us. We were born into the consequences of their choices and actions, and therefore should understand this principle.

Some have felt hijacked, through no fault of their own, by the bad choices made by their parents and so understand better than most that the things people do, don't just affect them, it affects the people that are yet to come through them. Equally, many can also thank God that they experienced the positive benefits of this principle. It works for good and it works for bad. The point is, it works! And this is what we have to start getting our minds around; our thinking must change. We are not here just to reach the people we see today but also the people in their loins, which are potentially a vast multitude.

The greatest battle

As I have been praying, studying and thinking about this concept, I have had a growing conviction that the greatest battle in our city is the battle for the control of the loins of the current generation. The greatest battle in our city is about who will have control over the people in the loins. Who is going to control their destiny? Who will control the outcomes? Who will shape the lives of the children in the loins of the people inside our city? I believe the *Battle for the Loins* is perhaps the greatest spiritual battle on the face of the earth. And as we develop these thoughts in the pages that follow, I hope you'll come to understand why I have concluded that the one who controls the loins, controls the future.

Think about it, our future church is inside people's loins. Your future church is within the loins of the people you are reaching in your community today. Its ultimate size is greater than all the people you can see or reach in your community today, it includes all the potential in their loins. So the battle to rescue lost men and women from the power of Satan and bring them to Christ today is a bigger one than you thought; it is also a *Battle for the Loins*, a warfare which has as its prize the countless unborn lives in the loins of these people. Armed with this understanding we can make a far bigger difference in our towns and cities than any short-term evangelistic strategy will ever give us.

Life begins

Let's think for a moment about the final stages of the process which culminates in the arrival of the people in our loins, that is the natural process of conception, pregnancy and birth.

When a woman is pregnant, she believes that the baby is already alive. She doesn't consider that the baby is about to arrive or about to start its life. The baby is already here and is as old as the time since its conception. A mother is also acutely aware that whatever she does while carrying the baby in her womb, can make a significant difference to her unborn child.

Now consider, if that mother attends church throughout the duration of her pregnancy, was her baby in church? And did the fact that the baby was in church make a difference to it? I believe it did. I believe that wherever she takes her unborn child, it has an effect on it, because the baby is a living, highly intelligent being, created to learn, grow and be shaped by the environment it is exposed to.

Abortion is obnoxious to us as Christians because we consider the baby to be a person from the time of its conception, a human being who already has destiny working in its life. The unborn child is not just an embryo, a piece of flesh, or something less than a real person. It is a player in God's cosmic plan as a potential surgeon, teacher, craftsman, pastor or prime minister. We see the possibilities and believe that whatever happens to that life while it is in the womb potentially affects its destiny.

Remember what happened when Jesus and John the Baptist came into each other's presence while they were still in their mother's wombs? The unborn children 'leapt' in the presence of each other![11] That was a supernatural response to each other while still in the womb because they shared a common destiny and purpose. John knew that he was going to serve the Christ who was in the womb across the lounge and leapt! Jesus, who had only just been conceived at that time, sat in the same room and knew that he was in the presence of greatness and would later say about John, *'there's none greater than John the Baptist.'*[12] In a few years time they were going to share ministry and destiny together and they leapt in anticipation of it. So, don't tell me that babies in the womb are not alive, have no intelligence or don't know what's going on. Similarly, don't tell me our children don't know when they are in church!

In my home church we have three main services per week. So, over a nine-month period it's possible for a baby to have been in church 108 times while in the womb. What a great thought! By the time it is born, it is homesick for church! The baby is craving for the presence of God by the time it's born because the mother had it in the corporate gatherings of the church for nine months.

So to all you Christian mothers out there, don't start missing church during the first year of your baby's life while you 'get used to being a mum'. That baby grew for the first nine months of its life in church. It's already familiar with the presence of God. It has ears, it can hear us all singing about God's greatness. So after the birth it's going to be perfectly at home in the same atmosphere as it was in whilst inside your loins.

Now we are beginning to think like God thinks. We must now think further about the possibilities of influencing the future generations of people locked up in the loins of the ones we are reaching before they get here. Like God we must think in generational terms.

Loins of origin

The first person to come to Christ in a family line becomes the spiritual 'loins of origin' for every other person that comes after them.

If you were the first to be saved and now have children of your own, you have started a new line which springs from the new 'loins of origin' your New Birth represents. You were the first to break the pattern of godlessness in your historic family line. You were the first to step away from a generational pattern of not walking with God and have, therefore, set a new precedent for future generations. You have forged a new beginning for all who will be born into your family line. They may continue to have the same surname as your old family line but they are not coming from the same loins anymore.

My children, for example, are nothing whatsoever to do with their non-Christian grandparents. They have a natural blood relationship with them of course, but I don't believe that blood is thicker than spirit. As far as I'm aware, there has never been a Scanlon like me before. I represent a whole new beginning, a new 'loins of origin' for a new spiritual line of descendents. As far as I have been able to ascertain, there has never been a Scanlon that has served God, loved God or walked with God, never. I am, therefore, the first of a new breed of people called Scanlon. The name's irrelevant, though it's good that we grace the name with this new dimension because it's been known for some other things over the generations! I am the first of a new breed. Glenda and I have become the new 'loins of origin' for that generational line. I am not a 'chip off the old block' I am a brand new block! Not that the old block is necessarily always bad, it just isn't saved.

If you did a Scanlon family tree, you'd find that when it came to me something weird happened on the chart. From me on it developed at two separate levels. The blood line continues as it has done for generations but above it a new, superior branch would be found, a spiritual branch which will now lead all my descendents back to Glenda and I as their spiritual 'loins of origin'. This spiritual branch will greatly affect the blood-line too, because the influence of the spiritual line will drag the natural patterns of the old blood-line up to a new level. After I am long gone, family historians will research the Scanlon line and conclude that, 'this boy went off and did things, said things and achieved things that no other Scanlon had ever done before.' Why? Because in Glenda and I, the natural line was transformed by a new spiritual beginning and our family line will never be the same again.

I am, therefore, not part of the extended family, I have started a new family line. I am not part of the old order, I am the father of a new order. I have done, achieved and become a brand new breed, just as you have as the first person to be saved in your family. Nobody has ever been like us before. When we came to Christ, we broke the mould forever!

Because some of you have not seen this principle before, you have had far more struggles in your Christian journey than you needed to. You have been hijacked by old family members who haven't yet realised that you and your family are a brand new breed of people, a new branch from their line. And you cannot inter-mix, intermarry or intermingle the two breeds; they have very different values, principles and standards. They are fundamentally incompatible.

So, about things you once saw eye-to-eye on you find yourself saying: 'We don't go there anymore, we no longer speak like that, we don't get drunk, we don't sleep around, we don't cheat, we don't lie, we're not dishonest, our children aren't rude or ignorant, we're not small minded, we're not penny pinching, we're not depressive; we don't do…' whatever the old line did. You've started a brand new breed of people and you must understand that. There's far more at stake than just a family bloodline, this is a major spiritual issue.

At the age of fifteen I broke from my family line and gave my life to Christ. Oh how I wish I knew then what I know now! It would have helped me understand some of the battles that took place in my life. A schoolteacher told me about Christ, I believed it, received Jesus and at that moment started, without even knowing it, a brand new line of people; they were in my loins. At the ages of sixteen and seventeen Glenda and I gave life to Charlotte. Charlotte was five months old when we got married. She was not illegitimate, she was born to a mum and dad that loved her - it just took us a few months to get our act together, organise a wedding and so on.

We had been together several years by that time but technically we'd had a bad start in life. People usually go on dates, then get engaged and then married. We just dated, had a child, then got married – we skipped the engagement bit altogether, though I have bought my childhood sweetheart several diamonds since then to make up for it!

Of course, I don't recommend that anyone else does it that way. We messed up; we made a mistake. What we did was wrong but out of something bad came something good. I didn't do what a typical Scanlon might have done. We stuck together and decided we would make a future together. Charlotte was the first-fruit of our brand new line both naturally and spiritually. But we seriously wondered whether or not we would actually make it. Would we be able to keep Charlotte? Would the social services think we were unfit parents and take her from us? We didn't have any money and nowhere to look after her. We were so broke that we lived with Glenda's parents in their tiny house for a few months, which was very gracious of them, until we could get our own house which was a dilapidated 'one up one down' with an outside toilet. And we could have done with a shuttle bus to the toilet! Thirty years ago that was the inauspicious beginning of our then family of three: Glenda, Charlotte and I.

I remember sitting with Glenda on a park bench during our school lunch break, crying our eyes out because we'd found out that she was pregnant with Charlotte. We didn't know it was Charlotte then but God did! We were weeping and wondering how in the world we were going to tell our parents. I knew my dad would kill me and that Glenda's mum and dad would be devastated. I remember the weight of that awful moment as we wondered what on earth would happen to us. But now, thirty years later, look what we were crying over that day? God knew that inside our loins was not only Charlotte but Bethan, Ruth and Esther too. Four beautiful girls that have been a blessing from God to us and to the lives of so many other people. Charlotte has gone on to serve alongside me in ministry and more recently we rejoiced in the arrival of our first beautiful granddaughter, Hope Cherish.

There was a battle going on for the control of my loins. One voice was telling me to try and get out of the problem and pretend it didn't happen; another was assuring me that we could work it out with God's help. It was a deeply spiritual battle as I reflect back on it, a battle for all these wonderful people who were in my loins. Maybe the devil had an inkling what was going to go on over my life because of prophesies I'd had and so on, I don't know. But the truth is that Charlotte was inside our loins and she represented something awesome for the kingdom of God and the nations of the world!

patriarch

From God's perspective, every child inside our children, and every child inside our children's children, are all ours. I am the Patriarch of this new line of faith, just like Abraham was of his. So, God doesn't just regard Steve and Mark, our two sons-in-law, as the fathers of their children, he also sees me as the Patriarch of the line of faith that began with my girls.

Mark and Steve were also the first to be saved in their families, so they also have the joy of becoming the first of a new line of faith. Like me, they are a 'new block', a new family tree, a new order. There's never been a Stevens like Mark and there's never been a Gambill like Steve. Their children will be a second generation of that new line. And the children inside their children, which are not even conceived yet, God already counts as being in their line! God's already got them on his mind and wants Steve and Mark to understand that what they do today will affect their grandchildren and great grandchildren! Future generations will either suffer or be blessed because of something Dad, Grandad, or Great Grandad did.

This principle will change your perspective on life today. It will influence the choices you make because you understand the generational repercussions involved. For instance, you may find yourself in a situation where you end up saying:

'I can't do that.'

'Why?'

'I can't do that because of my grandchildren.'

'But you're not even married yet!'

'I know. But I believe I will be one day and I'm thinking about my grandchildren.'

That will freak them out but it's the truth! It's time some of you teenagers started thinking seriously about your grandchildren. For example when the boy says, 'Will you sleep with me?' You reply:

'No, I'm not going to sleep with you, I'm not going to have sex with you.'

'Why, don't you like me?'

'Yes, I like you.'

'Don't you want sex?'

'Yes, I'm tempted just like you.'

'Then, why won't you sleep with me?'

'Because I'm thinking about my children and my grandchildren.'

'What?'

'Look, as far as God's concerned, those children are already in my loins, and I don't want what's in my loins to be damaged or get a bad start in life because of a decision I make today. Do you understand?'

He may do or he may not. But what really matters is that you won the battle for your loins in that crucial moment.

Learning to leave

Every first generation believer is faced with the challenge of how to handle the interface between the old family blood-line and the new spiritual faith-line. But few realise at that early stage just how critical their decisions are for those in their loins. One bad choice early on in your Christian walk can result in your children being born into something far less than God's best for them, as we will explore later on in this book.

For now though, I want to show you what Abraham had to do in that situation. Remember, he was the father of all who believe, he is our spiritual Patriarch and his actions resulted in our spiritual new life today. This is what God said to Abraham:

'The lord said to Abraham, "leave your country, leave your people and leave your father's household, and go to the land I will show you. I will make you into a great nation, I will bless you, I will make your name great and you will be a blessing. I will bless those who bless you and whoever curses you I will curse. And all the peoples on earth will be blessed through you.'[13]

This is the original promise to Abraham, the first person to believe in a God that his forefathers never knew. It was a major deal and has much to teach us about the battle first generation believers face when they come to Christ. It is important that we understand it so that we can not only help ourselves as first generation believers but also be better placed to help others who will become the first to break free from their godless past.

God told Abraham to leave three things, his country, his

people and his family. His *country* was a geographical location with its particular pagan-worshipping culture. His *people*, or kindred, were his people-group within that country. His *family* were his blood relatives, who were idol worshippers. God had great things for Abraham but it could not be fulfilled if he remained inside his old family line.

This leaving was not just physical for Abraham, no more than it is for us. His leaving was going to be total - body, soul and spirit - or it wasn't going to be leaving at all. He had to leave his family, country, nationality, culture, values and the ethos of life he'd been raised in. He had to leave it mentally, forsake it emotionally and break free from the habits and mindsets he'd been raised in. Unless he did all this, God could not use him.

No other generation has to listen and respond to the command to leave in the way that the first one does. In fact, the first generation does the leaving for every generation that will follow. They experience things that second and third generation believers will never have to battle with – these will have their own unique battles but they are quite distinct from the first generation's. The first generation has to break free from the shackles and dominance of their family's negative spiritual history, and all the future generations still in the loins of their 'Abraham' are blessed because of that leaving. For this reason it must be thorough and complete, yet worked out in a manner which as far as possible retains good relationships with the natural family. This can be quite a challenge, a challenge that is at the core of the *Battle for the Loins* as we shall see.

The scope and extent of this leaving can be seen when we consider that when God told Abraham to 'leave your family', he was also asking him to leave the economic system in which he'd lived for generations. In patriarchal times the extended family would have governed your life. If I was a furniture maker for example, I would have wanted my daughters to marry someone from a related trade so that as extended families we could together monopolise the furniture trade and protect our wider interests. So, if she married someone who was a timber importer, he could supply me at a cheap rate and I would supply him with good quality cheap furniture; we would work together like a small co-operative. This system meant that walking away from your family was like committing economic suicide. God was therefore telling Abraham to separate from being dependent on the whole economic system of the culture he was raised in.

Some first generation Christians separate physically from their families but are still dominated by them mentally, emotionally or even financially. Many, though separate, continue to be manipulated by an old family line that doesn't easily let go. I've counselled many newlywed couples who had left their parents physically but not mentally or emotionally and were now suffering from an 'interfering in-laws' syndrome. Their challenge became, if they didn't cut the apron strings from their unsaved parents and put their strength into their new believing family line, they would continue to be completely dominated by their old values and beliefs. This unhealthy control brings into the new family unit the contamination of the old family line and establishes it for another generation – it just pushes its way through until the children are born. Sadly, but of necessity, many of these children have been so determined to escape from the cycle of generational ungodliness that they have moved away to new towns and cities across the world. For them moving out of their parent's home was not enough, they had to put more physical space between them to ensure the new line of faith got off to a strong start.

So, the *Battle for the Loins* starts with a battle to break the old generational ties. It can sound easy but as many of you will testify, this is real spiritual warfare and requires a great deal of determination and wisdom to ensure that the new line of faith gets off to the strong start God wants. Victory is crucial both for you and the future generations in your loins.

[1]   Genesis 14:17-20
[2]   Numbers 1:47-53; 3:5-13
[3]   Hebrews 7:1-10
[4]   Hebrews 7:10 King James Version, Amplified Bible, New American Standard Bible
[5]   W.E. Vine, Expository Dictionary of New Testament Words, Oliphants, 1973
[6]   J.A Motyer, New International Dictionary of New Testament Theology, Vol 1, Zondervan, 1986
[7]   Romans 4:11-12
[8]   Galatians 3:9
[9]   Romans 9:6-8
[10]   Galatians 3:7
[11]   Luke 1:39-45
[12]   Matthew 11:11
[13]   Genesis 12:1-3

CHAPTER 2

The Battle Begins

Some time after I became a Christian, my mother went to see the Doctor about me! She had concluded that I was sick. She didn't tell me about this until many years later, long after I had left home. The story went something like this:

'Doctor, my fifteen year old son Paul is ill.'

And the Doctor said, 'What's wrong with him?'

'Well, he's … how do I explain this… he's changed,'

'Hmm. In what way?'

'Well, all of a sudden he's changed, become different. I mean, he's more honest! And he's started coming in on time and he never used to do that. He's even stopped swearing.'

Now that was a miracle! I'm not proud of it but I held the ten minute non-stop swearing record at my school, which is not easy. You have to think really hard and string the obscenities together in one continuous flow – I was an expert! But one of the first things that happened to me when I got saved was that I instantly stopped swearing. My mates tried to get me to swear by all kinds of devious schemes. They'd tackle me hard on the football pitch and so on. But I wouldn't, and it wasn't like I was trying not to, it just left me, it was supernatural.

Mum continued: 'He's stopped getting into fights too and is not as abusive as he used to be.'

'I see!' said the Doctor. 'And how is he doing at school?'

'Oh, much better' said Mum. 'He seems to be getting on a lot better with the teachers these days.'

No doubt the doctor's thinking, 'I haven't heard a problem yet', but lets Mum continue:

'And he goes to church now, three times a week. We think he's reading a Bible... it's in a cupboard somewhere... And we've caught him several times talking to himself in his bedroom.'

She was of course referring to my praying. Then the tone lowered and Mum swallowed hard before expressing the thing that had really freaked her and Dad out:

'What really worries us is that sometimes when we hear him talking, it's not English, it's like some weird thing he does... We've asked him about it and he said it was called speaking in tongues. But it is really bothering us. We think he's lost it mentally. I mean, who ever talks to themselves in a weird language and thinks it's OK? We really think he's ill.'

The Doctor paused and gave a long 'Hmmm.'

By the way, when they go, 'Hmmm' it usually means they haven't got a clue what to say but they're buying time!

His next probing question was, 'Does he have a girlfriend?'

'Yes, he has a girlfriend – but they're very happy,' said Mum.

'Ok. Is he doing exams?'

'Oh no, he's not the exam type I'm afraid. I don't think he'll do well in his exams.'

'I see' pondered the Doctor. 'Well, is he worried about anything?'

'Well that's just it' said Mum, 'He's not worried about anything.'

Finally, the Doctor sat back in his chair and after gathering his thoughts made his diagnosis:

'I've seen this before, Mrs Scanlon. Let me tell you what it is. It's a phase. Boys of his age sometimes go through phases like this. Generally they pass in a few weeks and he'll be back to his old self. Just give it a few weeks.'

Well, over thirty years later, this 'phase' is clearly terminal! And I'm seeking no cure!

When my mum first told me about that conversation I just couldn't believe it. However, it has lingered on in my memory as a pointer to just how radically saved I was. She did what she did simply because nobody in our family had ever been a Scanlon like me before. Nor has there ever been a person like the one you've become in your family as a first generation believer. And because they can't explain you by any reference to other family members, they may try to find medical terms to describe your behaviour! Such is the change that takes place when we are the first to get saved from a totally heathen background.

The Battle breaks the cycle

It is my joy to serve in a church where I hear regular stories like my own; tales of lives radically changed by meeting Jesus. And I particularly love it when young people come to Christ. They have their whole lives ahead of them; they have more chance than most to build up a strong momentum of godliness to pass on to their children and beyond. When they break the cycle, people really take notice.

One such young man, now aged thirteen, who comes from a very deprived home within our city, had major problems at both home and school. Teachers and parents alike did not have a clue what to do with him and he was eventually expelled from school. He first came to church on our buses about eighteen months ago, when he was just eleven. He gave his young life to Christ. Since then he has made massive progress in his life, both within his family and at school. He recently won an award for progress within his school, which was a gold award for being the most improved child in his year group. His three brothers, sister, cousin and grandma all now attend the church with him. He works on a team which helps the younger children within the church and has an awesome serving heart.

We snatched this young life from the devil aged eleven and he has begun to transform his family through his testimony. He has reached both forwards in time to his younger siblings and backwards to his grandparents. He hasn't shouted, preached or Bible bashed them, but for eighteen months he has simply lived a transformed life behaviourally. They have seen something in this young man's life that discipline and punishment couldn't touch. And this is what I mean when I talk about people being saved and breaking the generational cycle that has characterised their families for years. Who knows where that young troubled boy was heading? But now he's heading for a great life and so is everyone inside his loins.

Another young lady comes to mind. She came to church aged nineteen as a Mormon. A year or so ago she got saved. Since then her uncle has come through, is attending our Discovery course for new believers and has got really plugged into the church. Her four younger brothers now also attend with her.

Another teenager I can think of has, since she got saved, brought along her father, two uncles and her father's brother-in-law. Three of these men have all made firm commitments to Christ.

All these young people are the first line of faith from their heathen, unsaved family line. As the Bible says, '*a child shall lead them.*'[1] Each has become a catalyst for reaching their families and beyond. Their struggle to find their feet of faith has carried within it all these family members and all the future generations still tied up in their loins. They, like the point of an arrow, were the first to punch through their historic family's generational resistance to the gospel and create an opening through which others can now follow.

The battle breaks the strongholds

As we have observed, every single person is born into a culture which shapes their world-view. This was Abraham's situation and the essential reason God asked him to leave it behind for the promise-filled life that lay ahead of him. Like Abraham, we have all adopted value systems, attitudes and patterns of living without ever remembering where we actually learned them; they are just there in the atmosphere of our world and they subliminally shape our thinking. As a result, strongholds are established in people's minds and it is these which must be broken as part of the *Battle for the Loins*. Each newly saved person must get a strong start, be radically saved, completely turn around and change their thinking. By so doing, they break the wider circle of life patterns that have controlled their world.

When I mention 'strongholds' some of you reading this will

immediately think of demons, principalities and powers that your spiritual context has taught you can only ever be removed by loud and frequent intercession. But the strongholds in our cities are not demons that we need to shout at. I believe the strongholds in our towns and cities are entrenched ways of living, lifestyles, value systems and cultures. They are mindsets that children are born into and raised with. So, if they are raised around crime, violence and abuse they know no different. By the time the stronghold is passed to them it has the momentum of multiple generations behind it, and the baby born to that family and atmosphere today has got little or no chance, short of the miracle of a new start in Christ. So we have statistical repeat patterns all across our city, and indeed the world, of children who simply do what they see others doing: monkey-see-monkey-do! What you are raised in, you just tend to do; you know no different.

Dismantling the strongholds

These entrenched life-patterns are able to continue unchallenged from generation to generation because they have deep roots into our subconscious mind. If they were in our conscious mind, we may change or challenge them a lot sooner. The data in our conscious mind we can usually remember learning, or we can at least track it back to a clear source, so we are therefore in full control of what we do with it. But things in our subconscious mind have often been there for years, they are the product of prolonged subliminal programming entering our mind under the cover of tradition, assumption and culture. We certainly cannot remember where we learned them, they are just part of our family life, ethos, and value system. These are the true strongholds that must be broken as we fight the *Battle for the Loins*.

The Apostle Paul teaches how to dismantle strongholds within the context of a battle like the one we are discussing in this book. He wrote: '*The weapons we fight with are not the weapons of the world. On the contrary, they have divine power to demolish strongholds. We demolish arguments and every pretension that sets itself up against the knowledge of God, and we take captive every thought to make it obedient to Christ.*'[2]

I have observed that the process Paul presents here for dismantling a stronghold is also a description of the way a stronghold establishes itself in the first place, all we have to do is follow his advice in the reverse order. Much like building a wall, strongholds go up one brick at a time, and that's how they come down too!

There are four key thoughts to note from the passage quoted above. Together they provide us with the steps that combine to create or dismantle a stronghold:

Thoughts: Everything starts with a thought and over periods of time established thought patterns settle into established world-views and patterns of life. At one time it was 'only a thought', 'just an idea' which people went along with but today it is an established value within a family, organisation, church or wider society. Some thoughts are good, others bad. Some lead to life, others to death. But the mind is our starting place for everything.

Contradictions: Somewhere somehow a thought is challenged by another; a contradiction, argument or pretension appears. So for example, the thought that Adam and Eve would die if they ate the forbidden fruit was challenged by the contradiction, '*Did God say?*' and '*You will not surely die*'.[3] Now there is a battle raging in their mind. Who is right, God or Satan?

Imaginations: Now the mind gets busy expanding the contradiction and creating a whole imaginary world of what things would be like if the contradiction is true. Before long Adam and Eve had developed a conviction that the forbidden fruit was actually '*good for food*'[4] even though no one had ever eaten it to test their imaginary theory – it could have tasted bitter for all they knew! When our world of imagination so distorts reality that we treat the imagination as reality, we are in trouble. We are like those who treat TV soap opera stars as if they are real people! We are actually one step away from a stronghold in our mind.

Strongholds: Eventually the contradictory thought that threw us into a whole new world of imagination, takes root. It establishes itself as our subconscious reality and like a cuckoo, takes over the nest and begins to lay its own eggs. Now we start to live as if the imagination were true; we respond to life, situations and people in the light of the stronghold in our mind. We are in the grip of a stronghold.

This is how it works:

- **Thought:** Our neighbour's dog is friendly but barks a lot
- **Contradiction:** Our neighbour's dog is angry and will bite me
- **Imagination:** A dog bite can give you Tetanus which causes rigidity and muscle spasms, or even Rabies from which you can die
- **Stronghold:** I have a deep-seated fear of dogs because they are trying to kill me. I can't walk past one on the street and I even break out in a cold sweat when I hear one bark. We had to move to a house without any neighbours just in case they

ever got a dog! Thinking about it, I've no idea where this fear actually came from! Maybe I had a bad experience as a baby?

I have met people with all kinds of weird and wonderful fears and phobias and you'd be surprised just how many were unable to tell me where they came from. Strongholds like these are subtle, deep and life-dominating. They must be torn down. And these are precisely the kind of strongholds that every first generation believer is faced with as they fight the *Battle for the Loins* in an effort to break free from their godless past and establish a new line of faith.

Dismantling the stronghold takes these same key elements and works them in reverse:

● Take control of the process as a deliberate act of your will. Paul wrote: *'Take every thought captive and make it obedient to Christ'*. This is a command, something you must do. You are not at the mercy of your long-standing thought patterns, they are actually at yours! So, grab a hold of them and submit them to what Christ says about them in his Word.

● Resist the contradiction. It is a lie! What God says is the only truth that exists. The Holy Spirit will lead you as a new believer into *'all truth'*[5] and God's Word is the *'Word of truth'*[6]. Together they provide the new context and frame of reference for judging which thoughts to dwell on, and many of your old patterns of thinking rooted in your godless past will have to change. Paul called that process the *'renewing of the mind'*.[7]

● Refuse to let the contradiction develop. Instead, allow what God says about the situation to develop and shape your inner world. You are not now living in a false world of imagination but a world of truth, rooted in God's word and ways. And if '*you know the truth, the truth will set you free*,' said Jesus.[8]

●   As a result, new strongholds develop which are good ones. The old ones are replaced by your renewed, God-filled mind. No wonder you now think completely differently to your natural family line! They are still controlled by the strongholds that have shaped your family for generations; you have established new, positive strongholds which affirm your position in Christ, your hope for the future, your destiny and God's hand on you and all those in your loins.

generational choices

Dealing with strongholds like these is a vital part of winning the *Battle for the Loins*, a very important part. I have always been uncomfortable about much of the teaching about generational curses and have come to believe that the defining issue for the life of the believer is not a generational curse but their generational choices. What my parents did is irrelevant and powerless in the face of the new choices I can make as a New Creation in Christ. How tragic if the future generations in your loins were locked up by the same stranglehold of faulty mind-sets that had characterised your unsaved family line for generations. Prejudices, attitudes, habits, traditions and all that is considered 'normal' have their roots in generational choices like those required to demolish strongholds. But as first generation believers, we have to make some fresh choices, ones that will become the new godly hallmarks of our new line of faith.

Unfortunately, because some first generation believers will not trace and change the source of these wrong world-views, they remain in place, seriously weakening the new line of faith. If the devil can deflect us from ever tackling them, he has pretty much ensured that the strength of our new line of faith will be weak and probably fizzle out because of the incompatible mixture we allow to exist in our family. As a result, the 'sins of the fathers' stay alive and well, never challenged, just painted over by your new-found spirituality. They are like a back seat driver, forever applying the brake to all the new thinking, freedom and destiny God is sending your way. These 'sins of the fathers' are not a curse we inherit, they are the consequences of choices that others before us made. My better choices will create better consequences, which will ultimately hand an awesome legacy to my offspring.

I have observed that our enemy the devil will try and use three things like this to prevent us from conclusively winning the *Battle for the Loins*. They are three secret weapons used in his attempt to perpetuate the consequences of a negative history:

1. Mindlessness

Some Christians just never think! They never question, examine or explore the reason for things. So, nothing ever changes. They get saved but never beat the drag effect of their natural family's negative traditions, mind-sets and prejudices. These deep seated and hidden threads of flawed thinking are so difficult to trace that they give up and try to live with them.

This mindless abdication is guaranteed to lead us to defeat in our struggle to establish a powerful new spiritual family line. God gave you a new mind, so use it to re-programme the software and pass on sound, accurate and virus free God-centred mindfulness.

2. context

Satan's second secret weapon is context. The context you have lived in up to the moment you were saved has shaped your world. And it has done so without you even realising it for the most part. So, if the enemy can keep you within the same old context of relationships, family, mindsets and so forth, you are less likely to be open to a new thought or direction. Your historic context will act as the foot brake once again.

The story of the Ugly Duckling is the classic tale of the power of context over reality. All his life the little duckling has been abused, rejected and despised because he just didn't look like a duck. He was big and scrawny, walked funny and was shaped differently to his brothers and sisters. He was just plain ugly from a ducks point of view! Then one day as he was hiding his ugliness in the bulrushes near the riverbank, he saw the most magnificent, majestic creatures he had ever seen. A family of beautiful, long-necked white swans were gliding across the water. Against every instinct that the context of his troubled life had taught him – which was to stay in hiding and not risk further rejection – he found himself helplessly drawn to those awesome creatures. As he approached the swans he bowed his head in preparation for the usual onslaught of abuse, but none came. They seemed open to him and glided over towards him. And it was then, for the first time in his life, that he caught sight of his own reflection in the water. What he saw staring back at him was not a duck but a magnificent swan, just like those coming towards him.

His problem had never been that he was an ugly duckling, it had been that he wasn't a duck at all! Somehow a swan's egg got into a duck's nest and the power of context took over and shaped his bitter life as a misfit. Maybe that story describes your life too and the sooner you realise that the context of your past was a lie, and that you are not a duck at all but an awesome child of God, the better. Every day we reach out to many of life's 'ugly ducklings' in our inner city and it has become our greatest joy to swim towards them, not from them, and show them how beautiful the person is that God sees within them.

Never underestimate the power of context; it is one of the devil's best kept secret weapons in the battle for the liberation of people's hearts. It is for this reason that we must take charge of the context of our homes, lives and churches.

3. Learned helplessness

Thirdly, Satan subtly uses learned helplessness to undermine our progress in the conflict. Many of you have learned to live with failure, you think you are good at nothing in particular and everything you try always fades out into insignificance. As new ideas are suggested you heave a sigh and think, 'I tried that once and it didn't work.' You teach yourself that you are helpless to change your lot in life. You develop a mental stronghold that cripples you just like the man who had laid by the Pool of Bethesda for thirty-eight years trying to get into the miraculous waters and be healed.[9] His past failure had conditioned him into believing that he was helpless. So when Jesus came by and suggested a new approach, he launched into his well rehearsed speech of explanation about how he was helpless in the circumstances. But Jesus was not suggesting he did it the old way, he was making a new suggestion. And when he took courage and tried it, he was healed! Sadly, many Christians are in the same trap and closed to new thinking about their future or their ability to make a difference in their lifetime simply because they have 'learned helplessness'.

Much research has been done among long-term hospital patients in an attempt to understand how learned helplessness prolongs illness and even leads to premature death. It showed that patients who had given up and resigned themselves to die noticeably picked up when they were moved from the ward of terminally ill people to wards from which people regularly went home well. It all pointed to the human tendency to learn a form of helplessness which was suggested to them by a context of hopelessness.

Where in your life have you surrendered to helplessness? Don't waste another moment laying next to that 'pool' or on that 'terminal ward'. Get up! Take charge of your life and break free both for your own sake and that of all within you

The battle establishes a new family order

What we are seeing is that the only 'breaking out' that can make a lasting difference is a true conversion experience; a salvation encounter that truly revolutionises a person's inner world and breaks them out of their old way of life, even though they may continue living in the same old environment. They may still sleep in the same bed, do life with the same family and still be surrounded by a less than ideal situation but the difference is, they have changed. They are a brand new person from the inside out. They are no longer depending on any external programme to help them survive, they are dependant only upon a vital relationship with Christ and his people. They now go back into the community that shaped them and are able to start reshaping it. They walk as salt and light, and as ambassadors of the Kingdom of God. They are the pioneers of a new order, the new loins of origin for all who will follow.

I was very touched by the sentiments expressed by one of the young men in our church at his wedding. He is a first generation believer. At the reception dinner, when he stood as the Bridegroom to make his speech, he said to his natural family, 'Today I want to honour my church leaders who are sitting at that table over there. In case you don't know who they are, I want you to know that these people are my role models in life'. I thought, 'what a courageous thing to say in front of your family', because they were all there. He went on to say, 'I have a debt I owe to them that I could never repay. They have helped me to become a man of God, they've helped me to live a responsible life and encouraged me to live my dream'. I swallowed hard and watched the faces of his parents, 'I wonder what they made of that?' I pondered. Generations of his ancestry were sat there and he did something that no one had ever done before from that family line, he stood up in front of them all and effectively said, 'you are my family and I love you, but these people who I've only known a short time compared to you, have become my fathers and my mothers, my brothers and my sisters; they've become my new family.'

He had been the first to break from that unbelieving family line and become the loins of a new order. And when his father spoke to the assembled guests he observed that, 'we're out-numbered three to one' which was a comment on the proportion of church friends there when compared to natural family members. He'd observed that 70% of those at the wedding were his new spiritual family, the church. The new family were the dominating culture over the old family. Spirit had become thicker than blood!

It can be really hard where necessary to separate from blood relatives, from people you love. God understands that. On one occasion Jesus received a message from his mother and brothers who were concerned about him. It seems they had come together to take charge of him and take him home. But Jesus sent a message to them saying, *'Who is my mother, and who are my brothers?' Pointing to his disciples, he said, 'Here are my mother and my brothers. For whoever does the will of my Father in heaven is my brother and sister and mother.'*[10] He'd been at home for thirty years prior to this time and he was in effect saying, 'Mum, it's about time you let me go'.

No doubt some were shocked, particularly his family! But he was saying, 'I'm not coming home because this is my destiny. In fact, I've already left home Mum. I love you but I've left you not just physically but in purpose, call and destiny.' Jesus was sending them a clear message that he had left any family control behind and from that time on we have no record that his family tried to interfere with his life again.

Some of you reading this may need to do the same as both Jesus and the young man I mentioned above did. Maybe it's family, maybe it's someone in your circle of relationships or someone at work. It could be someone on the other side of the world who tries to dominate and control you. Whoever it is, you may have to make a decision to leave that influence and nail your colours to the mast for the sake of your personal destiny and that of those in your loins.

The battle is personal

I close this chapter with one final illustration from my own journey. In 1987 a recognised and trusted leader brought a prophetic word over my life. I've never built my life on prophecy and don't advise that you do either, but this word really helped me at a time of some confusion. It was all about the spiritual battle over my life in the invisible realm, which I have come to believe rages over the loins of every first generation believer in the world. The word from God described a 'wrestling' and wars that were going on in the heavenlies, the focus of which was what my life would potentially produce and become.

The story of Daniel sheds more light on just how great the battle is that rages in the heavenly realms over potentially significant lives here on earth. At one point Daniel was interceding for God's people and awaiting an answer, which was slow in coming. The reason? Some kind of heavenly warfare. An angel eventually came and told him, '*Since the first day that you set your mind to gain understanding and to humble yourself before your God, your words were heard, and I have come in response to them. But the prince of the Persian Kingdom resisted me for twenty-one days. Then Michael, one of the chief princes, came to help me, because I was detained there with the king of Persia. Now I have come to explain to you what will happen to your people in the future, for the vision concerns a time yet to come.*'[11]

Notice that the Bible says '*from the day that you set your mind*' not the day you put your hand up in a meeting or prayed the sinners prayer. A lot of people have made decisions for Christ who have still not 'set their mind' to serve him, to humble themselves and make a difference. I now realise that the day I 'set my mind' to give my whole life to God, to gain understanding and humble myself, my answer, my destiny and calling were released from heaven – just like Daniel's was.

In the first few months of my Christian life I led about twenty of my school friends to Christ. The church that I went to had no youth group until I brought them all with me. Now the devil doesn't like that! I had crossed a line and the battle was on. More recently, as we went through what has become known as our 'Crossing Over' period as a church, I experienced some serious spiritual attacks, it was as if the warring over my life in the heavenly realms intensified and I felt the weight of that for a season. Why? Because I had 'set my mind' on establishing and building the new church that we have now become, which was ultimately all about reaching the many thousands we are today.

You see, the 'wrestlings' and 'warrings' over your life will not just happen at conversion. They will happen from time to time when, during your journey in God, you really decide to lift your game, up the stakes, or break a containment. These major, life-defining moments are usually accompanied by new levels of resistance, and new devils seem to come with each new level you reach for. But for every new devil we seem to fight there's an even greater prize to apprehend, the prize of securing a strong spiritual future for the next generation. Does all hell seem to be breaking loose around you at the moment? Then something awesome is about to happen!

[1]   Isaiah 11:6
[2]   2 Corinthians 10:4-5
[3]   Genesis 3:3-4
[4]   Genesis 3:6
[5]   John 16:13
[6]   Ephesians 1:13
[7]   Romans 12:2
[8]   John 8:32
[9]   John 5:2
[10]   Matthew 12:48-50
[11]   Daniel 10:12

CHAPTER 3

Just imagine...

I hope that by now you are realising just how important winning the *Battle for the Loins* actually is. It is vital to the success of our individual family lines of faith as well as our corporate success as the church of God in the world. The battle involves war in the invisible realm, the dismantling of mental strongholds and establishing a whole new value system as a Christian, as we discussed in the last chapter. Like Abraham, every first generation believer has also made the break from their old natural family line, context, environment and value system. This was essentially a spiritual leaving but must also be mental, emotional and sometimes physical, as we described in chapter one.

In this chapter I want you to let your imagination roll a little. Having grasped the basic concept of thinking generationally and the importance of winning the *Battle for the Loins*, I want you to project your thinking forward into the possibilities that are the result of our victory.

As explained previously, I was a first generation believer. There had never been a Scanlon like me before and everyone who came after me in the Scanlon family line were born into a new kind of home. They were born into a life governed by new standards, values, and agendas to the one I was born into. And, as the first in that line, I had a struggle that none of my children, grandchildren, or great grandchildren should ever have to fight again. It is the same for all of you who were the first to be saved in your family line. You faced a battle that all those in your loins will never have to fight; you fought it for them, once for all time – if you did it properly! Therefore, the possibilities for God to work in and through your family are awesome. Just imagine what God can do through your radically saved children, grandchildren... and so on. They could include all manner of world shaping influences. What a thought! And what a provocation to make sure we win the battle completely and utterly in our lifetime.

Now don't forget that when I talk about a first generation Christian, I'm not talking about people who just go to church or are particularly religious. I'm not talking about people who may say, 'my grandad was a Methodist lay preacher and therefore I'm actually the fourth in line from him', when everyone in between were heathens. Neither am I talking about any weak attachment to the things of God such as the fact that, 'I went to Sunday School as a kid', or 'I was christened as a baby'. No, I am talking about a faith that breaks the line and cycle of unbelief. I'm talking about people who get radically saved, give their lives to the cause of Christ and serve him flat out for the rest of their lives. I'm talking about people who, as far as is humanly possible, influence every generation that comes from their loins thereafter.

Imagine Legion...

Imagine the difference that Jesus Christ made to Legion's children. Legion was a man who was possessed by at least two thousand demons.[1] He was a maniac, living among the tombs where he gashed and mutilated himself. He was out of his mind. Legion had been rejected and put outside of society because nobody could deal with him. So they chained him up and exiled him to live in a cemetery among the tombs on the edge of town, an area the community avoided for fear of his crazed ravings.

One day Jesus arrived in his town. And instead of saying, 'get a bigger chain and stronger medication', Jesus saw that inside Legion was an ordinary man who desperately wanted to be free. With his hair matted and flesh mutilated, looking more like an animal than a human being, he came running towards Jesus screaming. His arms were flailing everywhere and the chains that he had snapped, hung off his wrists. No doubt the disciples were getting back into the boat concluding, 'we've docked at the wrong place today!' But as they were engaging reverse gear, Jesus calmly stepped forward and Legion dropped to his knees and cried 'Jesus, please help me, I've been tormented all my life. Help me!'

The Bible says that by the end of that day Legion was clothed and in his right mind. He was unrecognisable, free, delivered and ready to serve God. He wanted to go with Jesus but he had a better idea: '*Jesus said, "Go home to your family and tell them how much the Lord has done for you, and how he has had mercy on you." So the man went away and began to tell in the Decapolis how much Jesus had done for him. And all the people were amazed.*'[2]

Notice, Jesus said to him 'go home', so he had one to go to, a place he'd not been to for years. Imagine what happened when he walked through the door that day! Imagine what happened when his children saw him, or his wife, his parents, brothers or sisters. Imagine what the townspeople thought when he walked into town with a haircut, looking smart and clean, with a calmness and a gentleness about him. What an impact he must have had on those communities.

We don't know what eventually became of Legion or how old he was when Jesus met him. But it is certainly not beyond the bounds of possibility that he had children and even grandchildren. Imagine telling that story to your children! Imagine Legion's children sitting his grandchildren on his lap and urging him to tell them his story. Maybe he would say, 'Not again! I'm tired of telling it and I don't want to scare them.' But they would press him as only grandchildren can and he would launch into the story. The amazed grandchildren would doubtless interrupt him with cries of, 'No way! You were living in the tombs? You're joking aren't you? You were living like an animal? No way!' And Grandad would say, 'It's perfectly true and I'm glad you didn't know me then. But because of what Jesus did for me no demon will ever bother you; you will never go a night without knowing somebody loves you; you will never try to end your life; you will never ever wake up in the morning and wish you hadn't. I did that for so many years but you never will.' Why? Because Legion was the first of a new line of people and he won the *Battle for the Loins*. On the day he believed in Jesus, everybody down-stream of him was given a new start.

Imagine The Lepers...

Imagine the difference Jesus made to the children of the ten lepers.[3] Lepers were forced to live outside their homes and carry a bell which they had to ring to warn people of their disease. As they approached they had to shout 'Unclean! Unclean!' They usually lived in colonies outside the city limits. As a community they were despised and rejected. You couldn't actually catch leprosy in the way they thought but they did not know that then. So their ignorance actually created even more suffering for the lepers than their pure physical illness.

Jesus came across ten of them who travelled together as a group. All of them had families, mums and dads who loved them; and no doubt some had wives and children who they had not seen for many years.

Then imagine the day when Jesus said to the lepers, 'be clean'. And as they followed his instruction to go and 'show themselves to the priest', they saw their skin recovering right in front of their eyes. They could see blemishes disappearing, lost tissue returning and healthy skin complexion returning. Imagine when they got to their various homes at the end of that day shouting a word they never dreamed possible, 'clean, clean, clean, I am clean! I'm a new person!' Imagine the difference it made to their children and the grandchildren that were inside their loins the day Jesus set them free. On the day they were set free, so were hundreds of others across their family networks, both those living and those yet to be born. On the day they met Jesus, all who would come through them in effect met Jesus. Everything bad stopped at Jesus and everything good began at Jesus.

Imagine the widow...

Just imagine the consequences for the son of the widow of Nain.[4] This widow had a young son who had died and it was the day of the funeral procession. As the coffin passed through the streets towards the burial site with the widow weeping over her son, Jesus entered the town. He walked into the middle of the funeral procession, touched the box - ignoring Old Testament laws which forbade it - and said to the corpse in the coffin, 'get up!' Imagine the reaction of people as the box started to move! That young man got out of the box, walked away from his own funeral back to the house and enjoyed his own funeral banquet.

Imagine the difference that day made to his children. They would never have been born if it had not been for that day. Imagine telling that story to your grandchildren. It would be never-ending! And just think how many embellishments would be added to that story over a generation or two! But the point is, the loins of that young man were saved not just the man himself. On the day Jesus raised him from the dead, everybody that would ever come into the world through him was also given life.

Imagine the prostitute...

Once, Jesus was the guest of honour at a banquet hosted by a leading Pharisee.[5] The Bible tells us that a woman who was a prostitute somehow gate-crashed the banquet. She made a beeline for Jesus and as she sat behind him weeping, her tears splashed down onto his feet. She then bent down and with her long hair began to dry his feet.

Jesus had not said a word to her yet, but the tongues were wagging! The religious people at the banquet were saying to each other, 'what is Jesus doing? If he knew what kind of woman she was, he would not have her anywhere near him. Doesn't he know that she is a well-known prostitute and he's letting her touch him? This is disgusting!'

Jesus looked at them and said, 'I know you think I don't know what I'm doing but I know all about this young girl. I know her life, I know her misery, I know what caused her to do what she's doing. I know the choices she's made. But I did not come to look after people who are well, I came to look after sick people whether they are sick spiritually, physically, mentally, or emotionally.' He then turned to her and said, 'you can go, your sins are forgiven' and the whole religious crowd took offence.

Her liberation from sin was the start of a whole new line of potential Jesus-loving, God-following disciples! The children and grandchildren in her loins would trace their godly heritage back to that moment at the party for generations to come.

Here in Bradford, two more working girls recently gave their lives to Christ in our church. If these young girls make it, imagine the difference it will make to the children they already have and others they may have in the future. Imagine the difference between being born into a lifestyle of prostitution and drug addiction, or into an atmosphere of violence, abuse and crime, and being born into a godly home that's surrounded by a church family and with a mum who loves and serves God. Imagine the different start that child has in life compared to the one their mother or father had. Then think of the children who will be born to those children, twenty years from now. That's the effect of winning this battle! It's only a short space of time before the generational momentum builds up. The grandchildren of a nineteen year old working girl that gets saved today will never ever know that their grandmother was a prostitute because by the time they arrive, their grandmother is such a powerful woman of God.

And going back to our Bible examples, what about Rahab? She was a lap-dancer in Jericho but one day she broke free from that lifestyle and reached out for a new start. Matthew's gospel tells us that she actually finished up in Christ's family tree of faith.[6] Whoever would have imagined that!

Just imagine...

Imagine the difference Jesus made to the man who had been crippled for thirty-eight years, lying on a stretcher next to the Pool of Bethesda.[7] Imagine the day when Jesus came and told him to pick up his bed and go home. As he spoke, strength came into his legs and when he stood up his legs supported him for the first time in all those years. Just imagine the difference Jesus made to the people in his loins that day.

And what about the dead, twelve-year old girl whose father, Jairus, was a leader in the synagogue?[8] Jesus raised her from the dead. She probably went on to have children of her own and just imagine the difference Jesus made to their lives that day. She would have raised them in an atmosphere of believing in the God that raised her from the dead because all of her life she was indebted to what he did for her that day.

Imagine the difference Jesus made to the children of blind Bartimaeus[9] who had been a blind beggar all his life. And what about the woman at the well?[10] So we could go on. The day all these people encountered Christ, so did everyone in their loins.

Imagine your city...

We are realising more and more that to make a difference to the generations yet unborn, the people responsible for rearing them need to have a strong walk with God. They must have a virulent strain of Christianity and an overwhelming love for Christ that shapes their world.

The sad truth is that even a Christian can still pass on poverty mentalities, fears and flawed values. Believers can pass on bad habits, cynical attitudes, negativity and rebellion. We can pass on non-worship habits, non-prayer habits and a lifestyle that doesn't live by the Word of God. And children growing up in this kind of environment end up living in a mixture, a watered down version of the real thing. They will need their own first generation experience because their parents live as if they are unsaved.

You see, in one sense the devil doesn't mind you being saved, he just doesn't want you making a difference to anybody else's life. We must realise that our battle is not just for 'bums on seats' or 'hands up' in a meeting, we are here to make disciples of the nations. We want people to make a difference in our towns and cities. We want the schoolteachers, governors, the courts, the police and social services to begin noticing the difference we are making. And what is it they will point to? Not speaking in tongues or church attendance. They will point to reduced crime, new standards of morality and behaviour, more responsible people, stronger marriages and families, and stable, sound young people who are reversing the trends of decay and deprivation in their inner city schools and communities.

The Bible says that *'when the righteous prosper, the city is exalted.'*[11] When we continue to prosper and are radically sold out for God, we become the devil's worst nightmare. The last thing he wants is for you to do something with the awesome power of God available to your life. He knows that if you start to think and live according to these generational concepts, his stranglehold on your city will begin to weaken. For that reason, he's quite content to contain you where you are. He doesn't mind putting you on 'hold' in a cosy church where you can have a great time, just as long as you don't help anybody.

But we see it God's way. We are the 'church in the city' and 'the city in the church.' We shouldn't be forever aware of where the lines are between the church and the city. We should be the church in the city and the city in the church, churches without walls of separation from those we are sent to reach.

So, you may be saved and in church but if you're not really growing in God and going for God, though your loins are Christian, your children will be born into 'form without power', which is religion. So the battle is not just about being a Christian. It's about being a Christian and pursuing your God-given destiny. People like this bless and prosper their city for generations to come.

Some of you reading this are now beginning to realise that when you have a 'bad day' and decide to skip church, there's a lot more at stake. It's a bigger issue. Your natural and spiritual children and grandchildren are at stake, and ultimately the very city you live in. If you play fast and loose as the first generation, the devil smiles ear-to-ear and says, 'That's cool! I hoped this would happen, I hoped that you would allow skipping church to be an option in your life. I needed that two months you took away from God's House so

I could get other voices into your life and other opportunities that would distract you.' Then before long, the months will turn into years during which momentum will be lost and all that will remain is a small spark of what used to be a burning fire. For you, missing church, allowing things to loosen you from the soil of God's House and going walkabout may be an option but for me it isn't. Because it's not just about you, it's about all those in your loins who need us to stay planted in God's House, for only there says the Psalmist, will our lives truly flourish.[12]

Eventually, as our city leaders and Governors see the positive influence of long-term generational thinking and working through churches in the community, they will start asking the people of God for help in the running of the city. Thus will Isaiah's prophecy be fulfilled that many will come and say, '*Come let us go up to the mountain of the Lord, to the House of the God of Jacob. He will teach us his ways so that we may walk in his paths.*'[13]

Imagine your nation...

Individuals combine to make a community, communities combine to form towns and cities, towns and cities combine to form a nation. Therefore, every individual has the potential power to influence their nation.

Here in Britain we don't really have any other type of people to reach than first generation believers because we are not a Christian country. The vast majority of people are unchurched, ignorant about the things of God and quite happy to tell you so. Therefore, the majority of people we reach today will have to face their *Battle for the Loins*, that's why it is so important that we understand its nature. And if further proof were needed, in a recent BBC programme entitled 'What Does the World Think of God?' Britain came rock bottom in almost every category of the survey's search for God-consciousness. We are a truly heathen nation and frankly I prefer it that way. At least the lines are clearer and we don't have the huge twilight zone of pseudo Christianity that some nations suffer from.

The *Battle for the Loins* is, therefore, the battle for Britain because we are not primarily dealing with millions of second generation Christians. In the UK, the chances are that if you go within a stone's throw of your church building and knock on six doors, every one of them will be the first person that has ever been spoken to about the gospel. Do that in many places around the world and you're going to find people whose parents and grandparents were Christians. But in the UK we are dealing primarily with potential first generation believers. So, the invitation to come to Christ also involves for them the first time 'mother of all battles', the *Battle for the Loins*.

from imagination to reality

I am told that our city's Royal Infirmary maternity unit is one of the busiest in the country. Over one hundred babies a week are born there. That's in excess of four hundred babies per month and over five thousand during the year. Doubtless, some of those babies were in the loins of some of the many thousands of people we reach through the various ministries of our church. Most of these people who come to Christ are the first generation to believe. So, generational thinking says that the baby born in Bradford Royal Infirmary today will get a better start in life because of something we did that touched its parents. We reached the 'people inside the people' when we reached that prospective parent.

Our Kids Church outreach is inspired by generational thinking. The nine or ten year olds who ride our buses to church today and give their lives to Christ will, within a decade or so, be the believing parents of the children that were in their loins the day we reached them. It is therefore well within the bounds of possibility that within a thirty to fifty year period, a local church that thinks and works generationally can begin to affect the spiritual balance of its community, tipping it in God's favour.

I am forty seven right now and have just become a grandfather. By the time our granddaughter Hope gets married, Glenda and I will only be in our sixties, so we will live to see at least our fourth generation being raised in God's House. We were the first generation, Charlotte the second, Hope is now the third and her children will be the fourth. Who knows, we may even get to see a fifth generation of the line of faith which commenced the day I was saved at the age of fifteen, thirty two years ago! By then I will have enjoyed watching each successive generation of my loins loving and serving God, and gradually influencing the community we live in. I can't think of a better way to go or a stronger legacy to leave.

As we continue to unwrap this concept I want you to understand that this is serious and significant business for our hands to be doing; this is the real deal. I'm praying that as I share these things, young people in particular will start thinking now about the generations in their loins. I pray that these thoughts will stop them doing anything that would prevent their children and children's children from getting a spiritual head start in life.

Through every young life we rescue in our inner city who is now growing up making different choices, we take more ground in the *Battle for the Loins* of our nation. The battle is on; it is a battle for the control of the future. It is a *Battle for the Loins* and we must win it.

[1]   Mark 5:1-20
[2]   Mark 5:19-20
[3]   Luke 17:11-19
[4]   Luke 7:11-17
[5]   Luke 7:36-50
[6]   Matthew 1:5
[7]   John 5:2-15
[8]   Luke 8:41-56
[9]   Mark 10:46-52
[10]   John 4:1-26
[11]   Proverbs 11:10
[12]   Psalm 92:12-15
[13]   Isaiah 2:3

CHAPTER 4

what you can't leave
is where you stop

Having let our God-filled imaginations roll forward into the awesome potential consequences of thinking in generational terms, I trust you can see more than ever just how important it is that we win at all costs the *Battle for the Loins*. The more I think about it, the greater urgency I feel to reach those in the loins of my community. And equally, greater is the righteous anger that wells up in me when I see Christians who are living self-centred lives without giving a thought for those who will be born into the consequences of their lethargy. So, before moving on to look more closely at the battle faced by second and third generation believers, I want us to examine more closely some of the potential reasons why we may not break from our past as thoroughly as we ought.

It is a principle of life that whatever or whoever you can't leave, determines where you will stop in one aspect of life or another. Whatever you can't separate from mentally, or whoever you can't uncouple yourself from emotionally, whether it is a girl, a guy, a divorce situation, a church, a bad experience, or whatever, that is where your life stops. It is usually easy to justify your decision to rest for a while in either spiritual or life-stage terms but the truth is you've stopped.

Have you ever been driving a car that keeps losing power and slowing down, maybe even to a standstill? You begin to think of all the things that could be causing it. Is it the timing belt, is the head gasket going, maybe it's the clutch? Before long you have convinced yourself that it needs a new engine! And then you realise that the handbrake is still on! You feel rather silly but with a sigh of relief release the brake and off the car goes.

This is what we are like in life. We sometimes don't feel we're moving like we should be, things are noticeably slowing down, or maybe they have stopped altogether. So we start to think of all the possible things that could get us going again. We decide to read that book the preacher recommended, to attend that conference we saw advertised, or to try and get time with the people we are sure hold the key to our breakthrough. Churches are the same too. They slow down, so the pastor begins to cast his eye around for the key to getting things moving again. How can he stimulate the growth that's dropped off and recover the momentum the church has lost? He concludes that the church needs a ministry like one he saw at a church in another part of the world, so he invites a team from there to come. Or he goes to the latest church growth conference and comes back with a file full of methodologies that he imposes on his weary people in an effort to kick start the church's momentum.

Both the individual and the pastor in these scenarios are looking at the wrong thing! Instead of thinking through every possible wild and wonderful option that may need to be added to fix the problem, simply start by having a look at what it is that is causing your life or church to stop in the first place. Why are you slowing down? What caused you to stop?

Take the brake off

In the process of crossing my home church over into the thriving church we are today, I realised that there were actually only a few things that were stopping us. But until I had addressed these, we would never leave the point we were fast slowing down to rest at. One of them for example, was control; we were a controlling church. We controlled everything as a senior leadership to ensure that the church was kept pure, that we knew who the members were and where they were, that the teaching across the church was sound doctrinally, that we were counselling into people's lives systematically, that our pulpit was a life giving platform, that every ministry was running smoothly, that the evangelistic teams were functioning, the creche was well equipped, the Sunday School had enough teachers, the car park enough marshals and the stewards all had a suitable name badge. We controlled it all, no wonder it slowed us down because we are supposed to be the pace setters for the church! As the senior leader in particular, I therefore came to see that if I wanted the church to grow, I had to move from controlling people to empowering them.

The problem was that I had been under a ministry for many years which itself had a controlling style of doing things, so I had to ask God to show me what to do. He told me plainly to 'let go of what's stopping you'. In other words, take the brake off! Not to do so would mean the church was in danger of perpetuating a second, third and fourth generation of 'locked up' controlled church. I had to become the first leader in that ministry to say, 'we're not going to have this any more, we're not going to be a controlled people anymore and as leaders we are not going to be controlling of the people anymore'. So, I let go of this controlling attitude and all the practical systems by which was maintained in the church structure, along with a number of other things that were making us stop. Overall there weren't many, but those few had a major drag effect on our progress until we let go of them as a positive act. Since then, it has been like travelling with the brake off!

It is vital that you identify the things that are slowing you down, hindering your momentum and acting like a brake. Until you do, no amount of new initiatives, ideas, anointed visiting preachers, books, conferences or church consultants will give you the elusive key to the new impetus you seek. It is not new impetus you need, it is the identification and removal of the things which are acting as a brake. Just think about it: if you try and impose more and more impetus with the brake still on, eventually the strain on the organisation or person reaches breaking point and you will have a major breakdown. Sadly, herein lies a reason behind many a church split and burned out pastor.

So, try and spot the things that are slowing you down. For example, when God says to you as the pastor 'do this' and you start seeing the faces of people who you know will disapprove, you have just identified one of the brakes. The brake has to be released, so let go of them, leave them mentally, emotionally and if necessary physically. They are simply intimidating and manipulating both you and the church into a 'parking bay' to suit their own personal agenda.

Unless you let go of what's stopping you in this way, you are in danger of becoming another generation who will do little or nothing for God. You'll be nice people, you'll love God and no doubt have a good life. But it will not be the great life you know deep down in your heart that you should have had, if you'd only had the courage to let go of the people and things that slowed you down to a halt.

sustaining momentum

Remember what God asked Abraham to do? He had to leave every influence that would stop his forward momentum so that he could use him for his greater purpose. It was crucial to him winning the *Battle for the Loins* and establishing a strong new line of faith. It is instructive to note where the impetus for his momentum in life actually came from because the same sources motivate us too. Momentum potentially comes from looking in three places: looking *inward* to see what Christ has put within us, looking *ahead* to where our vision inspires us to press towards, and looking *upward* to the things that by faith we sense God is wanting to send to our lives. The one place we never ever look for momentum is *backwards*.

We see this illustrated in the incident where God sent an angel to rescue Lot and his wife from Sodom. The angel told them, 'don't look back'. But Lot's wife couldn't resist a backward glance.[1] She had left Sodom physically but couldn't uncouple herself emotionally. So, she looked back and the Bible says that she instantly turned into a pillar of salt.

Don't let your past turn you into a pillar of salt. If you do not let go of what makes you stop today, you're in as much of a solidified, static and immovable state as she was. You can be frozen solid mentally, emotionally or spiritually, and still be in church with your hands up in the worship. And though you still tithe and do all the things that you used to do, inside you've begun to wither, shrivel and solidify. Whatever looks back in your life mentally, emotionally or spiritually will bring you to a stand still. You can be in a church, listening to preaching in an atmosphere that's forward looking, exciting and packed with impetus and momentum, but be totally untouched. On the inside you've gone on hold, like someone's pressed the 'pause' button and you're at a standstill.

So, what is slowing you down today? Whatever it is, let it go before you end up completely solidified!

Abraham's error

Going back to Abraham's story again, when God told him to leave his family, people and nation, he was almost fully obedient! I say 'almost' because the Bible tells us that '*Lot went with him*'.[2] We don't know how it happened but we do know it was in direct contradiction to what God had told him to do.

It's interesting to me that God never took issue with Abraham for taking Lot with him, even though he was disobedient. This teaches me that God will allow you to keep people involved in your life who you should have separated from for the sake of your loins and your new beginning in God. The choice is yours – you just need to be aware of the consequences. It seems to me that God was saying, 'Abraham, I told you what to do, but if you choose to allow a relationship that you should have cut off to continue into the new life I've planned for you, it's your decision, I'm not going to take issue with you'.

However, what did happen is that God went quiet on Abraham; he did not speak to him. For a prolonged period of time there was no more word from God. Through the silence God was saying, 'I cannot speak to you, and I will not speak to you about things to do with your destiny and my call on your life until you are fully separated from those you've included. I can't tell you about the things I have for your life because Lot will think he's included in it too, and he isn't, it's just for you. So, you have now slowed down the flow of my directive word to your life'.

Lot was only one man but one too many. He caused quarrels and great upset to Abraham and his household. He was a greedy person and his greed spawned all kinds of unrest and dysfunction in the family. Having Lot with him almost cost Abraham his life on one occasion too.[3] Lot's problems became Abraham's problems because he was family and all this should never have been taking place.

Please understand me: I'm not saying that we shouldn't have good relationships with our unsaved parents, brothers and sisters, grandparents, aunts, uncles, nephews and nieces – and so on. We should have a great relationship but we should never allow the ungodliness in any part of our blood relative families to dominate, control, dilute, destroy or pull us back from our commitment to the new life in Christ that we have chosen. All these things can become the brake that slows us to a halt. So, don't make Abraham's mistake, leave Lot behind!

who do you take with you?

When God tells you to leave someone or move on from something, he expects you to take full responsibility for who comes with you and who does not. That's what Abraham failed to fully grasp. Generally, we are better at including people than excluding them. But unless we become good at both, when from time to time God expects us to move on from something, we will miss it. It can be hard to exclude your blood relatives, it can get emotionally manipulative and you don't want the hassle or the upset. Abraham clearly had that problem.

But think of it this way: whoever the first generation bring with them has an effect on all in their loins. If they don't exclude someone they should have left behind, every future generation will be influenced by that inappropriate voice that lingers on as a shaper of their thinking, values and relationships. This is how big the stakes are for the first ones to believe.

Even if you get free and 'almost' fully obey God, the devil can use the little you bring with you that you should have left behind to tangle you up with emotional manipulation, guilt and mixed loyalties. He will let the 'little' sit there until eventually it spreads like a small piece of yeast that influences the whole loaf. And so it goes on until a generation or two down the line there's little observable difference between your new family and the ungodly one that you left all those years ago.

That's why God wants us to do all our leaving up front. We must do it at the beginning and be thorough, radical and ruthless so that we're not battling it later on when God is calling us to do something really important for him. When God says, 'this is the moment, you're on stage now, this is what you were born for', the last thing you want to be is hesitant, struggling, or confused. And all because there is something tucked away in your life that you should have left behind years ago. That small thing can place a warp in your soul, a doubt in your mind or a fear in your heart because of who you allowed to travel with you on the journey to the place God is calling you.

Some people leave our lives by themselves, others leave with a hint but some people need to be told flat out, 'you are not coming with me!' I believe that first generation believers must become strong at this. Otherwise, the people we're reaching today who have a lot to break free from, will get saved and be in church five or ten years from now but still not seriously impacting their own or future generations.

I guess we love including people because we all like to be liked. After all, it's not nice to say 'you're not coming'. There's also a good chance they will ask, 'why?' And then we are really struggling for some convincing explanations. Notice that God didn't say to Abraham, 'go to your family and explain all this, I'll give you two months to do it, then you can leave'. Abraham couldn't do it because he didn't have a clue what he was doing or where he was going! Which is another major challenge the first generation has that future ones don't. I couldn't explain to my unsaved parents and family where I was going in my new life. I had no map, like the second generation have, no means of assuring my family that I knew what I was doing. This is a journey of faith and faith does not see with the natural eye, but that is all the unsaved have.

In the past few years, particularly during our church's 'crossing over' period, I've had to sit with people and say to them, 'I love you and I really want you to make it but you're not coming. I don't want you with me as you are. I can't take you with me because of all the strings you have attached. I don't want you with me 'back seat driving' what God tells me to do. I refuse to have your critical attitude with me. I will not read anymore of your bad letters. I don't want you in church meetings, sitting there with your arms folded staring at me because you're upset by what I'm preaching. I know that if I don't say this to you, you will sit in this church for the next five years and the devil will use you to try and intimidate me. But I'm not going to let the devil or you do that to me, or this church. Hear my heart, I love you and I want you to make it, but you're not coming with me as you are'.

The book of Acts records an instance where Paul and Barnabas got into a strong dispute with each other about whether or not the young John Mark should go with them on a proposed ministry journey.[4] Paul was adamant that because John Mark had deserted the apostolic team on a previous occasion, he should not be trusted again. Barnabas strongly disagreed and was so sure that Paul was misjudging John Mark, he left Paul and set off on his own taking John Mark with him. The issue of who was right and who was wrong is not, I believe, the primary reason for the inclusion of this incident in Luke's record of the Acts of the Apostles. The lesson is that Paul took great care over who he allowed to travel with him in life and ministry, and so must we.

I came to realise during our 'crossing over' that some believers have no concept of the possibility of separation from certain past relationships if the purpose and call of God requires it. Most people in church life would rather live with a poor relationship that's lost its edge of purpose and politely endure it, rather than facing the issue.

On one occasion Jesus turned to the crowds and said, '*If anyone comes to me and does not hate his father and mother, his wife and children, his brothers and sisters—yes, even his own life—he cannot be my disciple. And anyone who does not carry his cross and follow me cannot be my disciple.*'[5] From time to time he deliberately said things to sift the crowd, many of who were only following him for their own personal gain. On one occasion he even put the same challenge to his closest disciples, just to make sure those he did want with him were there for the right reasons too.[6]

We used to have a dog called Jack. Whenever we left the home and didn't take Jack, he'd jump up onto a seat by the window and bark and bark. The only reason Jack barked was because he wasn't coming with us. He was a smart dog and tried to control us by barking because we were going somewhere that he wasn't. The truth was that if after we had left, another car pulled up with a total stranger in it, opened the door and said 'come on Jack' he'd have gone with them and been happy! And so would a bunch of people in the church! They're 'barking' because you're not taking them with you but its not really about you, they'll go with anybody. However, at the present time there's nobody else to go with, you're the best thing in town. So they are barking at you in an effort to control you. The truth is that if another church opened in town, some of those 'I can't live without you' people would leave you and go and join that church because it's not about you. It's about being with somebody that they feel would never do anything in life without them or pursue a purpose bigger than them.

Now a bigger problem starts when, as you drive off, someone in the car starts attributing human emotions to the dog. 'What a shame, he'll be bored and lonely, this is cruel! Look at him, he looks so sad, maybe he was abandoned as a puppy and that's why he's barking'. Then when you drive off you start worrying about the dog. As a result, your day is ruined. You've left him but he's still with you, dominating your thoughts and conversation. And in just the same way, that 'barking' person who you were supposed to leave way behind is now present with you in thought. That barking 'dog' is still controlling your life! Although you've physically left, your mind and emotions are still anchored to that 'dog' which actually isn't suffering at all, it is just angry that you dared to leave it.

Some of you will remember the old song, 'I have decided to follow Jesus'. It ends, 'No turning back, no turning back'. It's a great song, simple and true. Yet millions of Christians seem to have decided to follow Jesus as long as they can keep turning back; as long as they can keep 'Lot' with them, as long as they can keep a little bit of the past, as long as it doesn't involve upsetting their family or friends.

Don't forget, I'm not talking about leaving people in a bad attitude or in a wrong way. I'm talking about the kind of separation that destiny often calls for. I'm talking about separating emotionally, mentally and spiritually because you are either a new breed of person in your old family line, or your purpose is increasingly taking you on a separate path from the old church relationships you used to have. Compromise in either of these relationships can be fatal to our destiny.

Our start as a Christian must be clean, clear and uncluttered. Our resolve must continually be to look and travel in one direction only, forwards. Luke's gospel tells us that, '*As they were walking along the road, a man said to him, "I will follow you wherever you go." Jesus replied, "Foxes have holes and birds of the air have nests, but the Son of Man has no place to lay his head." He said to another man, "Follow me." But the man replied, "Lord, first let me go and bury my father." Jesus said to him, "Let the dead bury their own dead, but you go and proclaim the kingdom of God." Still another said, "I will follow you, Lord; but first let me go back and say good-by to my family." Jesus replied, "No one who puts his hand to the plow and looks back is fit for service in the kingdom of God."*'[7]

Jesus was making it clear that if these people were serious about following him, they would have to separate from some relationships. But they wanted the first thing they did as a follower of Jesus to be going backwards! How odd! If as a first generation believer, the primary pattern in your life is always to refer backwards, you are not going to make it through the *Battle for the Loins* to the establishing of a strong new line of faith. People who go back to try and sort something out usually don't return. They get so entangled in what they thought would only take a short time to sort out! Life teaches us that it is usually not worth trying to sort things out because your decision to follow Christ cannot be explained adequately to an unsaved mind. Sadly, I've seen many new converts never recover or return from going back to explain themselves to their families. This is because the approval they went looking for never came, so they stayed hoping it would come soon but it never did. Consequently, they never returned.

The Bogle family crime tree

The importance of thoroughly breaking the old, godless generational cycles which dictate the pattern for most people's lives, and starting a new faith-filled one, was brought home to me again through an article in one of our national Sunday newspapers.[8] It was a true story, describing the family tree of three generations of the Bogle family. The accompanying diagram showed, by a lock and key over each name, which of them were currently in jail or had been imprisoned for various crimes. Here is an extract from the article:

Liars, cheats and thieves all. Pa would have been so proud

Rooster Bogle rolled into Oregon in America's Pacific North-West in 1961 as a migrant farm worker from Texas and started his extensive - though not very rewarding - family business: crime.

Their family tree was uncovered by officials looking for ways to break the cycle of family lawlessness in the state. When they checked prison, probation and welfare files, they discovered that no fewer than 28 members of the Bogle clan were either in prison or had served sentences.

"Kids are so eager to please, they imitate their parents," said Fay Gentle, the training and transition co-ordinator for the Oregon Department of Corrections. "Instead of learning appropriate behaviour, children of people who go to jail are learning to cheat, lie, steal and manipulate."

Three generations of Bogles are now serving or have served jail sentences. Ms Gentle said that each Bogle currently in jail costs the authorities about $600,000 (£390,000) a year.

"Rooster raised us to be outlaws," said Tracey Bogle, 29, the youngest of seven of Rooster's children by his wife Kathryn, 55 - another two were by a girlfriend.

"What you're raised with, you grow to become. You don't escape." He acknowledged: "There's a domino effect in a family like ours."

Tracey Bogle is currently serving a 15-year sentence for kidnap, rape, assault, robbery and burglary, in the Snake River maximum security prison in eastern Oregon. He carried out his crimes with his elder brother, Robert Zane Bogle, who is also in prison, while their oldest brother, Tony, is serving a life sentence for murder in Arizona. Their mother was released from jail a month ago.

Allen Beck, of the Bureau of Justice Statistics in Washington, said that 47 per cent of inmates have a parent or other close relative who has, or is, serving a prison sentence. Half of all juvenile offenders have at least one parent with a criminal record.

Oregon hopes to break this crime cycle by establishing the family trees of all new convicts, then trying to intervene in families before more crimes are committed. They will offer treatment for drug and alcohol addiction and mental health problems, and training courses in "anger management" to curb violence.

The state has already started to keep track of younger members of families with criminal histories, watching out for signs of anti-social behaviour. Rooster Bogle - full name Dale Vincent Bogle - was a hardened, habitual criminal before he reached Oregon at the age of 20. He had been jailed in Texas, regularly beat his wife when drunk, and would send his children to steal from shops.

One Bogle has escaped the family legacy, or at least adapted it. Tammy Bogle Stuckey has never been arrested or used drugs, and is now the women's director of the **Stepping Out Ministry, a church-based group** running halfway houses for former convicts.

"It seems perfectly normal," she says of her work caring for paroled prisoners. "They're just like my family."

Sometimes, they are her family. Her son from an earlier marriage, Jason Bogle James, came to her after being released from a sentence for robbing a shop to pay for heroin.

She found that he was "not serious" about giving up drugs and crime - so she had him jailed again for breaking his probation. "I'm actually relieved when he's in jail," she said, "because I know he's not out trying to get himself killed."

Did you notice the paragraph about the one who got away? I am not sure the reporter fully realised the significance of it; three generations of crime cycle round and round and the only break was when somebody got Born Again. It took someone who was changed from the inside out to start a new line of Bogles.

As we have just read, correctional facilities and external programmes alone are not going to work. You can chain them, put them in jail, discipline them and remove privileges from them. But, if there is no change on the inside, the long-term difference in society that everyone wants, is never going to happen. The real difference we are after starts on the inside with a change of management. That is what beat the generational crime cycle in the Bogle clan. Tammy Bogel in effect said, 'I know that crime is all my family have ever known, but not me. I am going to break free from this family line and start a new one with different values.' Only the cross and the empowerment of being able to start a new life in Christ can break these generational patterns in people's lives.

Tammy Bogel has become the first of a new breed. Hers will not be an easy journey, she will have to fight and win the *Battle for the Loins*, she will have to separate appropriately from her godless, crime-ridden background, she will have to make frequent choices about who and what from her past can or cannot move forward with her. But if she continues to follow Christ, she will have started a whole new line of Bogels who will improve the world not worsen it.

master separators

The first person to believe in a family has to be a 'master separator', a master at cutting the strings and attachments to their past. As we have seen, God will not prevent us allowing people to come with us who we should have left behind. He may go quiet and postpone saying some things until we've cleared up who should be on the journey with us. God reasons that if the loins are not safe, he cannot begin building this new line.

For Abraham and Lot things came to a head through a quarrel between their families and staff, and they finished up separating. It is noticeable that after this event we read: '*The Lord said to Abraham after Lot had parted from him...*'[9] It was now safe for God to speak to Abraham about things which did not immediately include Lot.

Parents, have you ever wanted to get the children to bed so you could have a talk about something it would be inappropriate for them to be around to hear? Have you ever wanted somebody out of the way just so you can say something? Maybe it's exciting news, something you want to say but it seems like every time you're just about to say it, somebody is there who shouldn't be!

You're almost bursting by the time you get to say it! God was like that with Abraham, he was bursting to say more to Abraham than 'leave' but when Abraham left and retained mixture in his life, God couldn't. I don't want God to go quiet on me because I've kept something or someone in my life that I shouldn't have.

I believe there are things God is waiting to say to some of you and he cannot, simply because the wrong people are close to you. If the seed is not safe and prone to contamination due to relational compromises then God will wait. Let's pick up Abraham's story again: *'God said to him after Lot had gone, lift up your eyes from where you are, look North, South, East and West, all the land you see I will give to you and your offspring forever. I will make your offspring like the dust of the earth. Go, walk through the length and breadth of the land because I'm giving it to you.'*[10] It was always going to be about more than just leaving his family. But until he finally left properly by separating from Lot, God couldn't tell him the next amazing things he had for his life.

Like Abraham, we must become 'master separators'. It takes skill and wisdom to handle some of the relational consequences of leaving your past behind but the rewards are enormous. 'Master separators' are very successful in the *Battle for the Loins* because they have understood that nothing must hinder their own strong start or be allowed to carry through and contaminate the strong start of those in their loins. 'Master separators' understand that even along the journey they may have to shed some relationships, attitudes or mind-sets that become brakes on their momentum. They understand that what they can't leave determines where they will stop.

All the leaving's done!

It is interesting to note that God never asked Isaac or Jacob to leave anything. He never asked them to leave their country, their father's household or family because Abraham was expected to do the leaving for all in his line. The first generation 'leave' for everyone, 'exclude' for everyone and suffer for everyone. The first generation therefore endures the pain and suffers the abuse for doing these things for the benefit of the second, third and all subsequent generations that follow them. First generation believers are the 'punch bags' on behalf of all who will follow. They take all the heat, abuse and punishment from those who misunderstand, persecute and resist them in their natural families.

Speaking as a first generation 'punch bag' I want to assure you, it is all worth it! Just consider what it meant for my children. It means they will never suffer for going to church like I did. They will never be persecuted for daring to get serious about God. They will never be forbidden to play Christian music in the home, like I was. My children will never be forbidden from having their Christian friends over. My children will never be teased, abused and sworn at just for carrying a Bible out of the house and walking down the street with it. They will never experience the pain of their family disowning them as they left the house for church, nor the loneliness of returning to a house where God was not to be mentioned.

Gladly, my children will never ever experience any of that, which is fantastic. But I did. I was increasingly aware that I was battling things uniquely as a first time believer, that I was in a spiritual war for more than my own soul or sanity, it was for all those in my loins. Some days it would have been easier to put the Bible away, to cut down on church attendance, to not put any money in the offering, sing any worship songs or ask if I could have a friend round. It would have been easier to live a double life. But I was so serious about God that I didn't want to compromise!

I have observed that some second generation believers know

how to live a double life simply because they've been around both. I was only around heathenism and so never knew how to 'play church' and look like an angel in the meeting but live like a devil the rest of the time! I had no background to help me so I just lived fully for the new life I had found. I knew the difference between my past and my future, being lost and found, loving God or ignoring him. And for me, there was nothing in between. So I was unusually radical in my commitment.

Only now do I realise that all the battles I fought and the trouble I had were part of a war over my life and the destiny of my offspring. At fifteen and sixteen years of age, when I was going through some of those agonies, I didn't know that one day I and my children would be touching the world! I didn't know that I'd one day lead an awesome church and be writing a book like this. I didn't know any of it but God did and the devil probably had a vague idea too!

I left for them

Writing this book has caused me to look back and reflect much on my childhood. I have then had the joy of turning to look at our children and the great life they've had from day one. They have been raised in church, able to worship, enjoy living in the supernatural, pray and see miracles happen. They've been able to live in a God centred home and bring their Christian friends round. Because God's House was in our house, they have also grown up planted among some great people. They have been in countless meetings, known the presence and power of God and the atmosphere of heaven here on earth in the only church they have ever known. They have seen us tithing and giving our money into the Kingdom of God. My children and now my children's children, will never experience the *Battle for the Loins* that I fought and won. They will have their own challenges and battles but they will never be a 'punch bag' for the devil, who knows that if he keeps losing the *Battle for the Loins*, he may end up losing an entire generation.

So, it's awesome that my children will never suffer what Glenda and I did. It's awesome that our children will never be able to say, 'I don't know where I'm going'. They know where they are going because we have given them a map! All four of them are now second generation believers, born on their way to a God-given destiny. They were born on the way to somewhere, born into purpose and pilgrimage like the children born to Abraham, Isaac and their succeeding generations. But someone had to do the leaving first; someone had to be the 'Abraham' at the head of every godly family line.

The challenge is now for the second and third generations to keep following the map we gave them. Abraham is described as the 'father of faith' because he set out not knowing where he was going, much like I did and like many of you have. To use the Star Trek analogy, I 'boldly went where no Scanlon had been before'. Now, for those who follow, it becomes a journey of following in the footsteps of their father's faith, further establishing the line of faith and making their own unique mark on their generation.

[1]   Genesis 19:26
[2]   Genesis 12:4
[3]   Genesis 14
[4]   Acts 15:36-41
[5]   Luke 14:26-27
[6]   John 6:61
[7]   Luke 9:57-62
[8]   The Sunday Telegraph, 25 August 2002. Reproduced with permission.
[9]   Genesis 13:14
[10]   Genesis 13:14-18

1973

'MAY YOU REJOICE IN THE WIFE OF YOUR YOUTH'

PROVERBS 5:18

1973

OUR FIRSTBORN CHARLOTTE

SECOND GENERATION

The second generation's battle:

The Battle
for the BRIDGE

CHAPTER 5

The Battle for the Bridge

Having established the fundamental importance of winning the *Battle for the Loins*, which is the task of first generation believers, I now want us to look a bit more closely at the unique battle faced by their children, second generation Christians. My children are second generation, so I have been able to examine at close quarters the contrast between the struggles they have faced in their Christian walk and my own personal experience. It has been very different, as I have explained to some extent so far in this book. I also work and minister in an environment where my colleagues in full time ministry and our wider church leadership are a mixture of first, second and third generation believers, so I have had much opportunity to observe, research and discuss our respective journeys.

What's very clear is that the second generation have their own unique challenge. They are the children of radically saved first generation believers who, if they did their job properly, have established a strong new line of faith into which these children have now been born. So, they have a certain degree of generational faith momentum behind them but also they remain only one generation away from their unsaved family and the old way of life which that represents. Most will therefore have the challenge of embracing the faith their fathers raised them in but also still have to deal with some influence and potential pull from their grandparents generation.

Then, when you begin to think forward, they have the challenge of raising their own children, the third generation, in an atmosphere and context which builds on and adds impetus to that which they inherited, walked in themselves and are now passing on. I have therefore come to call the battle of the second generation the *Battle for the Bridge*. Their unique struggle has as its goal the challenge of bridging the generations either side of them. The first generation fought to break its unhelpful ties with their non-Christian past, the second generation fights to preserve and continue their faith-filled ties with their fathers generation. It is a completely different kind of battle as we shall see, and one which I am sure many of you reading this will identify with.

There can be a certain nervousness that attaches itself to the second generation. This has its roots in the unspoken fear of their spiritual fathers that if they don't make it, all that the first generation fought for will be lost. It makes the first generation nervous when they see second generation believers taking things for granted which they fought so hard to obtain. But maybe worst of all is the frightening prospect that if the second generation rejects God, there is no bridge to connect the line of faith to the third generation and beyond. We are back to square one and the *Battle for the Loins* will have to be fought all over again.

The second generation's *Battle for the Bridge* is fought primarily in the arena of identity. They want to be distinct and not just blend in with what their parents did, though they cannot deny that their parent's faith was awesome and has left them a great legacy. They want to establish their own faith and to be making their own choices, but they cannot get away from the truth that the best choices they can make are actually the same ones their parents made before them. Second generation children raised in a Christian home and church environment will find themselves asking, 'why am I here?' and questioning whether they really want to be there. Their battle is to find their true identity as a significant bridge between the first and third generations in this new line of faith.

weak bridges

Sometimes when you are out driving you will see a road sign that says, 'Danger: Weak Bridge'. It directs vehicles over a certain weight on to a different route to their destination beyond that bridge, usually a much longer one! And so it is for the generational line of faith if the second generation proves to be a weak bridge. If the first generation raise their children in the faith but they then don't follow through, the line is broken. So, we lose about twenty years of momentum, because in chronological terms a generation is about twenty years.

Now the first generation believer is the grandfather to a potential third generation grandchild, but the people who have most influence over that child is the generation closest to it, the second. So now it's virtually impossible for grandfather and grandmother who won the *Battle for the Loins*, to be close enough to their grandchildren and school them in a way that bypasses their second generation parents. This scenario occurs in many families and can create a lot of heartache. Sometimes, for example, the second generation keep the grandchildren from their own parents because they know they'll take them to church. This frustrates the first generation because they know that something has been lost that they fought and suffered for. The bridge has gone and there's no line for their faith to travel through to touch this third generation. What usually happens is that the third generation, who have been raised in a home with weak, diluted or no faith at all, has to start all over again. They have to fight the same battle that grandad fought, the *Battle for the Loins*. This breaks their heart because it is re-fighting a battle that should only be fought once.

In the UK today we seem to fight the same battle over and over again, and all because we have not thought or lived with these generational principles in view. We have not understood the power of momentum. A third generation child could be born into forty years or more of loving God, walking by faith and being planted in God's House. He's got forty years of faith beneath him and sometimes overwhelming him like a great supernatural tidal wave. That's why, as we will explore in the final section of this book, the third generation's battle is with 'the force of inevitability' that says to them, 'you haven't got any choice but to walk in the faith of your fathers, resistance is useless'. But if the bridge is weak or broken, momentum is lost and we end up re-fighting the *Battle for the Loins* again and again, in a cycle of generational failure.

The stakes are high in every generation. But all you second generation Christians who have parents who loved God and raised you to do the same, if we lose you, the loss of momentum you create has serious implications for you and all in the loins of your parents. So, I appeal to you as a first generation believer, on behalf of all other first generation believers: do not lose what we fought and suffered for. You have a huge responsibility to be faithful with what the first generation battled for and won. You must be God's bridge.

Blowing up the bridges

The first thing to be bombed in a military conflict are the bridges. So, second generation believers, you are under fire! Why? Because bridges are short cuts, bridges unite otherwise distant shores and form vital routes of communication, supply, connection and flow.

Without a bridge, you have to go the long way round to get to the other shore. And if God loses the bridge of the second generation, he also has to go a long way round. He has to wait years before he can now approach the next person in the loins and give them an opportunity to come to know him and serve him. So, if we keep the bridge in tact, we maintain the momentum. If we keep the bridge, the gap between the first and the third generations is virtually zero. It's like a seamless flow of life that goes from the one who won the *Battle for the Loins* right through to the generation of permanence.

The devil is after the bridges. If he loses the *Battle for the Loins* he will go for the bridges. Remember, he doesn't need to separate you from both ends, just one. You don't need to take a bridge out at both sides, just taking it out at one end means it's still lost as a bridge. He doesn't need to separate you from your children. If he can just weaken you from your parents, he has already separated you from your children in terms of a continuous line of faith. If he can weaken you from the parents that raised you in God, he has already loosened you from one end of the bridge. By the time you are rearing the third generation, there's no bridge. There's nothing coming over. The first part of the bridge is down.

Or conversely, if you retain a strong link with the first part of the bridge, your first generation, but are not careful in raising your children to appreciate the God of your fathers, he has bombed the other end of the bridge this time. There is still not enough momentum to establish the line in a permanent way. That's why we've all got to be so careful how we bring up our children. We must realise the awesome power of generational momentum. The devil understands the power of generational momentum and uses it for evil, as in the case of the Bogle family who we read about in chapter four. Therefore how much more with us.

second generation struggles

I am not a second generation believer but I can understand and appreciate the struggles of the second generation from watching my children's journeys, and from observing many other second generation people in the church. I've learned that they have some distinct struggles to work through to ensure that the bridge they form between the generations stays in tact.

One of the second generation journeys I have been able to examine more fully has been that of my friend and Associate Pastor, Stephen Matthew. Stephen and I have been in ministry together for over twenty years. Our journeys have been along the same road for much of that time but our personal battles have been radically different. I have fought the *Battle for the Loins* and he has fought the *Battle for the Bridge*. We have learned much from each other's journey and our respective experiences have contributed to our wider understanding of the principles we are exploring in this book.

I have therefore asked Stephen to share some of his experiences as a second generation believer in the section that follows:

what is normal?

In the previous chapters of this book, Paul has described what for him was normality. The normality of his home life was to be persecuted for his faith. He had to stand his ground and break free from the opposition that came from his family and friends as he started a new line of Scanlons. No doubt many of you, like me, have laughed to yourself as you read some of the stories he has told so far in this book. Many of you have identified with Paul and thought, 'yes, that's exactly how it's been; the *Battle for the Loins* is my battle.'

But I'm reading this thinking, 'No, not me. No, it was never like that for me'. Why? Because my battle was different. Let me describe to you the 'normality' of my upbringing. My dad was radically saved during the Second World War when he was in his mid twenties. He was a deeply committed believer until the day he died in 1996. He was a senior leader in the Brethren assembly that I was brought up in. When he was fifty-nine, God baptised him in the Holy Spirit – an amazing thing for a Brethren man - and God set him on another path. As a result, he helped bring the majority of that small church into the beginnings of what is today the Abundant Life Church. So, to me, he had a kind of founding father influence on this great church that we are a part of today. It doesn't look very much like it did then but, generationally speaking, there is continuity.

I'm one of four children and my older brother and two sisters were all part of the church here too. We were raised in God's House and enjoyed a wonderfully happy, stable and godly home life. Today, three of us are serving God in full time ministry. We are the enduring heritage of our parent's second generation, a heritage of godliness and passion for Christ and his Kingdom.

My Dad loved Paul Scanlon and one of his abiding joys, just before he died in 1996, was that I was about to come back to Bradford and work with Paul again after a few years ministering elsewhere. He was thrilled to bits that I was coming back to work with Paul and be part of building the church here. And I believe that is significant in the context of the generational principles we are considering here.

So my normality was: I went to church. I went to church four or five times a week. I was raised in Sunday School, prayer meetings, Bible classes and Gospel meetings. Our family home was where all the guest preachers came and stayed over. My Mum and Dad had an almost constantly open home, and it was full of evangelists and preachers and teachers. They all came and I got to know them all.

In our home I never heard a swear word. I never saw my parents argue, ever. And I believe that if you ask my children, today, they will tell you it is very rare that they have ever seen my wife Kay and I argue too.

I was saved when I was nine years old because an evangelist stayed at our house and one evening he led me to Christ. I remember kneeling by my bed and saying, 'Lord Jesus, come into my life, I give you my life,' and I prayed a simple prayer. I knew what I'd done. I got baptised and it was normal, wonderfully normal. There was talk of God in my home. It was just normal. I've never seriously strayed from my faith. I've never drunk alcohol to excess, never taken a single drug, never seriously smoked and never slept around. I've never committed a major crime, maliciously exploited anyone or lived a 'double life'. That has been my normality.

familiarity breeds...

As you can see, Paul and I have backgrounds that are about as different as you can get! But it is a generational thing, because my experience is now his children's experience, and so it goes on down the line. The truth is however, that I have had some battles! Big ones! And Paul's phrase the *Battle for the Bridge* is a great way of describing mine.

If I can put my battle into one word, it's been with familiarity. It has been with just taking God, church and this good, stable, moral upbringing totally for granted and thinking, 'isn't this a boring way to live!' That has been my major battle.

For people like me, the world has a certain attraction. Sin seems really exciting. It looks and sounds as if it's going to be the best fun ever. So the big challenge for the second generation is, 'will they or won't they' take the faith of their fathers so much for granted that they throw it out of the window. If they break the bridge we're back to square one. And the more Paul has developed the teaching in this book, the more grateful I've become that I did not allow the bridge of my life to be 'bombed' by familiarity.

As I have thought through my journey and the Battle for the Bridge of my life, I have identified three particular battles, all linked to this familiarity issue, which all second generation believers have to win.

The battle for personal faith

The first is that I had to battle to develop my own strong faith and not just ride on the faith of my parents. Having parents who are well known in the church can get you places! I was 'Reg's boy' and could get into meetings and hear things my peers were excluded from. I could get favours from people because of whose son I was. At one time my older brother, David, was an elder in the church too. So for a season I was 'Reg's son and David's brother', pretty good street-cred in our church context at the time!

But God brought me to a place where he challenged me about my own personal beliefs and reason for being in church. What did I really believe? I was good at parroting the opinions of others I had heard. But did I actually have an opinion of my own? What about when my parents die? What if I lost all my friends? What would I have left? God challenged me over a period with questions like this and I had to go on a journey to get my own 'roots of faith' established. I had to get into God's Word myself, have my own prayer life, have my own devotional walk with the Lord, and get to the place where I was so rooted in my own faith that I could grow strong.

Once I'd won that battle, once I'd battled through and got my own faith, the brilliant thing was this: the environment that I lived in made it like a greenhouse! I grew fast, because I had godly parents, brothers and sisters, and church friends all around me. I'd got a church around me. So I grew fast because I had decided, 'yes, I am going to go for Jesus,' and got my roots down. So I broke the familiarity thing firstly by developing my own strong faith.

The battle with inferiority

The second battle I fought was with inferiority. And I've found this to be true for lots of second generation believers. You see, if you line up a first generation believer and me on the platform and ask us both to give our testimonies of salvation, who has the better tale? He may tell you about his life of violence, crime, sin and debauchery, and I'm going to tell you what a good, clean living boy I was! And what's going to inspire people more?

I remember going to hear Nicky Cruz, who features in the book The Cross and the Switchblade, speak about how he led a gang in New York. He gave his testimony of killing people, extortion, drug and alcohol excess and so on. We were all gasping in awe. But at the end of it, I felt depressed! Why? Because I thought, 'he has been saved from so much more than me. Did I even need saving? Am I worth as much to Jesus as Nicky Cruz?'

So I felt inferior and I had to battle with it. Eventually, I came to understand that I was as 'hell bound' as anyone, Nicky Cruz or the worst sinner imaginable. I was as lost in sin as them and needed saving as much as them. In fact, I'd actually been 'doubly saved' because I'd been saved from all the pain they went through! I'd been saved from abusing my body with alcohol, cigarettes and drugs; I'd been saved from ever getting a sexually transmitted disease, a criminal record or custodial sentence. It's awesome! And that is why I am so grateful to be a second generation believer.

So, today I've got a strong root of faith and am so glad that I didn't have to go through the pain of many first generation believers in order to learn the joy of being saved from sin. Once I'd won that battle, I realised that I am as saved as the worst sinner and don't have to feel inferior to anybody.

The battle for confidence

My third fight was the battle to become confident enough to actually relate to the unsaved.

As Paul has mentioned elsewhere in this book, when we crossed this church over into the thriving outreach centre it is today, a lot of people left us. It coincided with the time when we started busing in a lot of unsaved people from some of the poorest housing estates in Bradford. And a lot of those who left were from my generation in the church; second generation believers who had become very comfortable with living in what had become something of a Christian ghetto.

Like them I realised that if I wanted to, I could live in a totally Christian world and never, ever speak to an unsaved person. My family were saved and so were the people I worked with. Most of my friends were saved. In fact, did I know an unsaved person? Did I want to know one? Well, no, they're dirty rotten sinners aren't they?

Second generation Christians tend to pull back a little from the world around them and feel, 'it's safe here in our nice Christian world?' So I had a battle to be confident enough to believe I could be used to reach the unsaved, they were like aliens to me, especially some of the homeless and hurting souls we started bringing into our events. How could I ever relate to them? What would they want with me?'

Kay and I are so blessed to be in an environment today where, as second generation believers, our four children are all saved and plugged into this same church with us. They are the third generation from my Dad's line of faith. And now we are Grandparents too. So in this House of God, in which my Dad was a founding influence as a first generation believer, I serve as a second generation believer and have the joy of seeing my children and grandchildren being raised in the same line of faith. The 'bridge' is strong, the battle for it won, and the legacy of my father's faith moves forward through my descendants towards permanence. God is so good!

I remember when Stephen and I first talked about our respective experiences and I asked 'what are the things you struggled with?' and, almost without hesitating, he said, 'I just felt that I never had a good sin!' I thought, 'I just can't relate to that!' What our respective stories do show is that each generation not only has its own battle but that each is also vital to the success of our corporate mission of reaching the world and raising a generational tidal wave of successive believing generations that will sweep over our cities and change them long term.

So, second generation believers, we understand that you are short of a good sin! We understand that this can be a pressure to you. But what the first generation are saying to you is, 'believe me, sin is not what it is cracked up to be!' As first generation believers let's continue to celebrate that we got delivered from sex, drugs and rock and roll! But not forget to also celebrate that the second generation *didn't* do that. Rejoice that they can stand up and say, 'The worst thing I've ever done is drop litter, and I felt awful about it! I've never done all that sinful stuff but I've wanted to serve God from my youth. I've wanted my destiny to be deeply tied up with God's kingdom, I've always loved the church, I've always loved the worship, I've grown up loving the Word of God. I've prayed and walked with God all of my life, and it is the best life ever!' Who wouldn't want to have a testimony like that? This is the testimony of the second generation who have won the *Battle for the Bridge*.

CHAPTER 6

Use Your Today To shape Their Tomorrow

Central to the concepts we are discussing in this book is the truth that what we do *today* will affect both our natural and spiritual children *tomorrow*. An awareness of this must be on us so that we take proper responsibility for all those future generations who will be affected by what we do. In particular, those faced with the *Battle for the Bridge* cannot escape the responsibility of ensuring they make conscious choices that create a strong bridge over which they can drive truck loads of spiritual principles and life-skills on which the third generation will thrive. They must use their *today* to consciously shape the third generation's *tomorrow*. The thoughts in this chapter therefore have relevance to both first and second generation believers because each are using their *today* to shape the lives of the *tomorrow* generation. They also relate to churches who in each successive generation have a responsibility to ensure that they are living in a way that leaves a legacy for those who will come after them in their community.

I'm sure that as you have begun to think more in generational terms through reading this book, you will have made some kind of conscious decision to ensure that you deal with any large, life-shaping elements that would hinder the flow of blessing from your generation to the next; things like addictions, immorality or foolish decisions that obviously have a long-lasting impact on your family line. But we must look deeper. Things that look innocent on the surface and therefore like something we don't need to bother about, can actually be more harmful because of their hidden nature. For example family traditions, which may have been good generations ago but today have no rhyme or reason whatsoever.

Sadly, the church is one of the best places in the world to find things being done for no reason whatsoever. The church is riddled with traditions that are not helping anyone and which few understand. Sometimes, even the people keeping the tradition going don't know why they're keeping it going, they're just doing it! We must resolve not to pass on to our spiritual or natural children any traditions that are irrelevant because they will only serve to give them a wrong concept of God. We must beware of burying God in tradition, religion, language and forms of expression that mean absolutely nothing to the current generation.

Dare to ask 'why?'

A newly married couple started life together and one day the wife decided to cook her favourite dish for her new husband, hoping it would become his favourite too. The dish included a big joint of ham, cooked just like her mother used to when she was a child. She prepared the ingredients and just before putting the ham in the pan took a cleaver and hacked off the end of the ham shank, and put what was left in the pan. On observing this, her husband said:

'Why, if you don't mind me asking, do you cut the end off the ham before you put it in the pan?'

'I've no idea' she replied.

'Why do you do it then?' he further enquired.

'Because my mother always did it and you haven't tasted ham until you've tasted hers.'

That was her definitive and final answer. But unsatisfied with this and now increasingly curious, the husband pressed it further:

'I don't want to be awkward or cause a domestic crisis here, but why don't you ask your mother why she did it? There must be a reason for it, otherwise it seems like a waste of ham to me.'

So she rang her mother:

'Mum, when you cook my favourite ham, you always cut the end off it don't you.'

'Oh yes' she replied, 'every time without fail.'

'I thought so! Can you explain why though?

After a short pause, Mum said:

'I don't know, your grandmother taught me to cut the end off the ham.'

So, no wiser, but now almost as inquisitive as her husband, she rings Grandma:

'Grandma, why did you always cut the end off the ham?'

'Oh that's simple' said Grandma, 'my pan was too small!'

That was it! There's no great culinary secret behind this tradition, just a small pan. But today you can get large pans. So, for three generations the end of the ham was wasted simply because grandma's pan was too small.

Now think church. When you politely ask the question, 'why are we doing this?' you discover it is riddled with things that exist for the same reason the ham shank was cut off! 'We've always done it this way' is the standard response. 'But why?' And before you know it, you are branded a subversive rebel in the congregation.

When we reinvented our church a few years ago, we learned to question a great many methods and mind-sets that were strongly rooted in our church and local community. We wanted to transition our children's ministry into larger groups from a traditional small-group format: 'Oh no you cannot do that' we were told. And some left over it!

We wanted to build a 2000 seat auditorium to be our main worship space. 'Never!' we were told, 'no one will come!' When we asked 'why?' the answer was, 'well, nobody's ever done it before'. But that's not a reason! That's like saying the pan's too small! Why can't we build a mega-church here in Bradford, in the north of England?

We wanted to have a huge Gift Day, a great offering through which people could gladly contribute to the proposed new building and pledge to support it over the following period. Our target was half a million pounds. 'What! You must be joking. You can't do that.' Again we asked 'why?' only to be reminded that we were only a few hundred in number and not based in the wealthy Stockbroker-belt of our country.

Today, we have a large, thriving children's ministry and a 2000 seat auditorium, financed initially by that 'ill-advised' offering which raised £620,000 – far in excess of our target. And all because we dared to ask, 'why not?' This generation must be prepared to ask the hard questions to ensure that the future generation in our loins never inherit traditions and mind-sets which are well past their usefulness.

Dare to tell the truth

Do you remember the story of the Emperor's New Clothes? In it a young boy was watching the parade. When the emperor came by he was completely naked but everybody pretended he was in his new clothes and said, 'Isn't he grand! Isn't he fine! What beautiful new clothes he has on today.' But the little boy said, 'The emperor is in the 'altogether', the king is naked!' And the crowd tried to silence the boy because he was shattering the politically correct illusion. He wasn't mature enough to pretend; he just knew it was a shambles and somebody should say something.

I have felt like that boy on many occasions during the last few years as we effectively planted a new church from within our old one. The process demanded we ask the hard questions about why the church was like it was; why we did things the way we did and even why we believed some of the truths we preached and practiced. Time and time again I would be presented with the argument that, 'If we change that, we will really upset some people. So best to leave it well alone.'

These were times for truth telling, not for dancing around people's particular likes and dislikes. So I would press the scenario further: 'OK, so they won't like it. Then what happens?'

'Well, they'll get upset and might leave the church' was a common reply.

So I would press further: 'Right, and what happens after that?' The truth is that we would just keep going, we'd keep pressing on outworking the commission we have to build this thriving city centre church and become a resource for the wider Body of Christ. People just needed to hear the truth, believe it and not let fear or people's small agendas hijack the whole church.

'Oh, you can't go on TV, whoever heard of a church from Bradford going on TV? How silly!'

So again I said, 'why not?' and pressed for the truth, for real answers with substance. Today, millions of people around the world have been blessed, reached and helped by our TV ministry which people said we couldn't, shouldn't and weren't qualified to run. I am so glad I did not listen to that lie.

In churches across the world today there are things being

allowed to continue that people put up with and tolerate. This is how irrelevant traditions are perpetuated and why churches stay small. Of course, if the issue involved drugs, alcohol or immorality many would stop and say something for the sake of their children. But all the while they are turning a blind eye to countless other things which are killing their church. They think their traditions are harmless enough but those things that we tolerate now will eventually become yet another reason why our children and children's children stay away from church.

We must have the courage to change our churches today and rescue them from becoming irrelevant to tomorrow's generation.

Be determined to understand

I was raised in a male chauvinist environment and it didn't help my worldview. That's why I think God gave me four daughters! Mind you, I've often treated my girls like boys. We'd play football, wrestle and generally 'rough and tumble' together. We had fun! But I think that God has worked on my life for over thirty years now, by surrounding me with women in my home because I was raised in a male dominated environment, one permeated with wrong ideas from earlier generations.

On reflection, most of my family have not even thought about where these chauvinistic traits come from. But I have had to because of the work of God in my life. I realised that being the 'macho' man and ordering the women around did not contribute to a happy home life. So why did my parents live like that? Because their parents did, and so on back through the generations. It didn't help my grandparents or parents and it hasn't helped some of yours either.

Our challenge is to understand ourselves, to realise where our attitudes to life have their roots and be prepared to change them for the sake of future generations. In this way we use our today to shape their tomorrow.

Teach the enjoyment of life

I was raised with a poverty mentality because we were in poverty. I was a post war baby and there was lack and deficiency. Many of you were too. The watchword in our house was, 'we can't afford it.' It was always 'going to be a bad Christmas' and it was only March! We grew up in an atmosphere of lack and insufficiency, always having more 'week' left than money. We were broke.

I know that some people think that being poor and not having nice things is somehow godly and befitting a Christian. I can assure you, it isn't. There's no virtue in poverty. I was raised with it and it took me years to break free from it. In fact, I still remember wrestling with it only a few years ago. The symptom I observed was that for all my life I never had the mental release to order dessert in a restaurant if I knew I couldn't finish it - unless I could convince somebody to share it with me, or make myself sick trying to clear the plate! My upbringing was engraved in my mind. I could hear my mother saying, 'waste not, want not, there are people starving in the world today! So, clear your plate!' In our house, putting food into the bin was a cardinal sin.

Later in life I began to realise that what my mother had been saying in my formative years about waste, was never about waste, it was about money. We couldn't afford to order anything and see it go to waste. But today, if I want to I can. So I said to myself, 'this isn't about waste this is about new freedoms that God has given my life. It's about having the freedom to make some choices I couldn't when I had nothing.' I realised that I had lived inside the containment of this seemingly small thing but that it had affected me almost daily. I haven't taught wastefulness to my children but I have taught freedom from any poverty and penny-pinching mentalities.

The full enjoyment of life requires you to ask yourself questions about things you are not actually thinking about. Think deeply and ask yourself where your attitudes and world-view come from; beware the mindlessness we talked about in chapter two. For example, why don't I look some people in the eye when I talk to them? Why do I always apologise, even though I've done nothing wrong? Why do I always say 'no' to the children on that particular issue? Ask yourself 'why?' and examine it thoroughly. And when you track it down, you'll find that in many cases there is no valid reason why you should live that way, think that way or behave that way. So, don't let these things detract from your enjoyment of life today because your breakthrough will bring freedom to your children too.

Whether you are reading this as a first or second generation believer, the mould your family line came from has been broken, all of it. So let's not pass on a mixture to our natural or spiritual children. '*Those who the son sets free are free indeed*',[1] free from everything and anything that would dilute the quality of your life today and therefore detract from the next generation's ability to enjoy life to the full tomorrow.

Teach life skills

For over thirty years now, Glenda and I have had the privilege of putting things into our children's lives that we did not want them to struggle with later on. We used our today to shape their tomorrow by deliberately teaching them God's ways and giving them life skills we believed would stand them in good stead long after we have gone. For example:

● Generosity

We have taught our children generosity. I love generosity. I love being generous. I love being a blessing in someone's world. It's now a way of life for us to be generous in our relationships and friendships; generous with our finances, gifts, abilities, home and hospitality. Generous people change lives and situations. Generous people are attractive and generosity grabs God's attention. Generous people think bigger and achieve more. Generous people can influence a workplace, school, university or city. So, model generosity to your children.

● Manners

We've endeavoured to teach our children manners and how to be polite, because I believe this is an important attribute that will serve them through their lives. It may seem so small but the well-mannered will always win the day over the rude and ignorant. The righteous have great manners!

● Hospitality

We taught our children how to be hospitable by always having our house filled with people. They saw us share what we had with our guests, even when we had very little. Some of you plan to be hospitable when you get rich! Don't wait, it may never happen. Just share what you have now.

Some friends once invited us to their home and we said that we'd love to come. Then they said, 'no, we can't have you yet.' So I said, 'OK, just let us know when you are ready.' Six months went by and they'd occasionally say, 'we're going to have you round soon.' Another six months went by as we waited until the kitchen was decorated and finished, then for the new furniture to arrive, then the back bedroom to be finished (though we weren't going to dine in the back bedroom as far as I knew!), until the garden's landscaped and then … Needless to say, it never happened. Remember, people aren't coming to your home for your cordon bleau cooking but your friendship and company. As the scripture says: '*Better a meal of vegetables where there is love, than a fattened calf with hatred*'.[2]

Hospitable people build hospitable churches and God sends the unloved and unwelcome to those places. He sometimes sends angels too![3]

● initiative

We taught our children initiative. We taught them that very often you can do something about the things people tell you that you can never change. I lived much of my life inside the prison of 'I can't change this' and have come to realise that I can, if I will just have the courage and take some initiative. Initiative is the power to start, stop or change anything. People of initiative are the 'head and not the tail'. These people run the economy, they rule and win in life. What a legacy to pass on to your children!

● Dignity

We taught our children dignity and told them, 'don't let anybody treat you like trash or walk all over you'. Several times throughout our children's school life, I ended up having to go to the school for a 'showdown' with a teacher who was bullying and publicly humiliating them as a form of discipline. Those shows of support helped their dignity and taught them to defend those less able to defend themselves in life. My father would never have stood up for me like that but I'm a new breed and we will live with dignity and treat others the same.

● confidence

We taught our children confidence. God cannot use anyone beyond their level of confidence; Moses, Gideon, Jeremiah, Timothy and others affirm this principle. We have endeavoured to steer our children away from shyness and silence towards confidence and contribution. We encouraged them to enjoy adult company and also to participate in adult conversation, especially as they approached their teenage years. We encouraged them to have opinions and voice them and not to back down or be intimidated by the stronger personalities in the room.

Achieving big things in life will require confidence and we, the church, have a massive job to do. So let's work to remove the crisis of confidence that seems to pervade much of the church today, particularly among our young people.

● prosperity

Something else we have taught our children is prosperity. The gospel improves lives. People get cleaned up, think better, dream bigger, make wiser choices and so they do better in life – including financially; their standard of living goes up because they are going up.

I used to be proud of my working class roots; I was ignorant, unsophisticated and proud of it! But there's no virtue in that mindset. As God has prospered us, we have taught our children to always be themselves but to enjoy nice things without feeling embarrassed about them or becoming materialistic. Many poor and working class people are envious and critical of people who have nice things; it eats them up. We had to defeat that in ourselves first and then pass it on to the children.

Some Christians are embarrassed by their nice things. So they come to church in the old car and leave the new Mercedes at home! They don't want people to think they are 'worldly.' But worldliness is not about doing certain things or having certain things, it is about an attitude to life and the way you live life. I am the first Scanlon to really prosper beyond a certain level. I want my children at home and church to see this and expect the same for their lives. After all, a financially broke church cannot help a city. Three of our children have just moved into beautiful new homes, they are way beyond where we were at their age and I take great pleasure in that because I started it all when I won the *Battle for the Loins*.

Teach spiritual habits

In addition to these life-skills and attitudes, we have also taught our children many spiritual habits, things like being involved in the House of God. Our children were raised in church, so in one sense they never chose to go, they were taken. But when they reached their teens we explained to them the importance of making their own decision to be a part. We said to each of them in turn something like: 'Mum and I were the first believers in our family and now you're the second generation. We've taken you to church all your life but we're not going to do so anymore. No longer will we shout for you three, four, five or six times to tell you we're going to church. From now on you've got to be there on purpose, not because we dragged you out of bed! You've got to want to be there and get yourself up, just like you do for school. In fact, school's far less important than church. School isn't teaching you things that will change your life and destiny like Church is. So, if this is as important to you as we believe it should be, you need to get up, get ready and be there.'

Of course, we had a few Sundays when some of them didn't make it and they soon realised we meant it. We therefore established that, just as they had chosen God for themselves, they must now choose to get fully involved in the life of the church. This then develops to include a choice to be a worshipper, a choice to love God's Word and develop great Christian friendships.

We also taught our children good giving habits. When they started being given spending money, we taught them all how to tithe – by doing it for them! We took their tithe off them for a period to get the principle in place, and helped them see how God was blessing them as a result. Then we asked them to choose to do it, something they have never struggled with since, it's established in their spiritual DNA.

It is therefore our responsibility to shape a generation, to teach our natural and spiritual children things today so they don't have to battle with them tomorrow. By doing so we can release them from many of the struggles you and I had and pass on to them a great legacy by teaching them these simple but important things.

The single christian parental influence

I am conscious that in most of the examples I have used in this book so far, I have assumed there are two Christian parents shaping the life of the next generation. This is not of course true in every situation. There are many single parent families thriving in churches today and equally there are families in which there is only one believing parent in the home, which is probably the more complicated situation to deal with. When only one parent is a believer and the other one isn't, it can be really hard to raise children in a Christian culture, with churchgoing habits and godly morals. It's not easy but it's not impossible.

I'm sure some of you in this situation think it would be wonderful if you were in homes where both parents were Christians. But I can assure you that they too have their own problems in raising their children to be godly. So don't think it's the worst deal in the world to have one parent saved and one unsaved.

Where you are the lone Christian parent, your task is to make sure that as far as is possible, the dominating culture of that family is a godly one. When Paul wrote to Timothy about his ancestry of faith, he never mentioned a male person at all. He said, '*I have been reminded of your sincere faith, which first lived in your grandmother Lois and in your mother Eunice and, I am persuaded, now lives in you also.*'[4] He didn't mention a father or grandfather, just the female line, as though nothing spiritually significant came into Timothy's life through male figures.

So please don't feel that this doesn't apply to you if you are the only Christian in a marriage situation. You still have all the opportunity, all the authority, and all the power in God to make sure that you raise that child with godly values. Make sure you school them in godly living, steering them away from attitudes and mind-sets that are not acceptable. Make sure it's your influence that takes them to one side and lets them know we don't do or say that in our family. Make sure it's you that protects them from imitating the behaviour of others around them that may hijack their beginnings in life.

The principle works

As we have explored aspects of how we can use our today to shape tomorrow for future generations, it has struck me again that these principles work whether or not we actually co-operate with or understand them.

Doing nothing today is shaping your natural and spiritual children's tomorrow just as surely as doing all the positive conscious acts we have been discussing in these chapters. It was wise King Solomon who noted:

'I went past the field of the sluggard, past the vineyard of the man who lacks judgment; thorns had come up everywhere, the ground was covered with weeds, and the stone wall was in ruins. I applied my heart to what I observed and learned a lesson from what I saw:

A little sleep, a little slumber, a little folding of the hands to rest - and poverty will come on you like a bandit and scarcity like an armed man.'[5]

The lazy sluggard did nothing but his vineyard was still full. It was full of weeds, thorns, thistles and decay. Imagine his son inheriting this mess. One would like to think he would have been appalled and proactively got on with restoring the walls, tilling the ground, planting new seed and establishing the vineyard as a fruitful place once again. But would he? In that he had been brought up in his father's house maybe he was a sluggard too! You see we pass on what we are whether we are aware of it or not. And if we do nothing, we pass on the mess and decay that results from doing nothing.

As I reflect back on my childhood, my father did actually pass a legacy on to me. He passed on all that he had, which was a certain set of values and attitudes which I subliminally adopted and had to break free from as part of my initial *Battle for the Loins*. To this day I don't think he deliberately set out to give me a bad start in life, he was just himself. In many ways I look back and think that he did very little but it is not so much in what he *did* but what he *was* that shaped me. As a man, the male figure in my life, he shaped me into his own image without even trying.

For example, implicit in the way he ran our home was that he was the boss. So, after I got saved and was told the Bible teaches that men should be 'the head of their home' I instinctively reverted to the model I had lived with. But he was a dictator! It was not until I was invited into other Christian homes that I began to see a different kind of headship and manliness modelled. I can still recall some of the early 'culture shock' I experienced as I did this. I saw a Christian man helping his wife around the home, washing up and picking things up and was astounded. I was thinking, 'What is he doing?' Why? Because I was raised in a macho, male chauvinist home where the women did all that kind of work. Then I saw this man show open affection to his wife, just a moment of tenderness like holding her hand, a hug, a smile or a kiss. I just watched, wondering what on earth he was doing because it went against the grain of my upbringing but was actually very heart-warming and reassuring. But could I do that with Glenda? I was quietly having a revolution and being schooled by God to be a better husband.

My point is, the principle works. You are using your today to shape their tomorrow whether you realise it and co-operate with the process in a conscious way, or not. The last thing you want is for your natural or spiritual children to be just handed all that you are without thinking, acting or consciously helping them to take your new line of faith onto a higher level. That's why it is such a joy to me that my natural children are succeeding beyond the level we did at their age. And equally, in the church I love it when young men and women with a passion for God step out in faith and do exploits for God which would have been beyond me at their spiritual age.

The second becomes the first

Finally, a word to any second generation Christians who feel that they have not been shaped as they should have been. If you are reading this as a second generation Christian and you started off with parents who were on fire for God but now they're not, then you have now become the hope of the loins of that family. It now falls to you to make a difference. Don't wait until your parents kick back in; don't wait until they get back on fire for God like they used to be. It has fallen on your shoulders to make sure that the line of faith that started with your parents, but is now not being continued through them, is able to continue strongly through you.

In many ways you have now become a first generation Christian, not the second, by virtue of the fact that you need to stand in this line of faith for your children's sake. You need to have such a strong dose of God that by the time your children come, they can look to you for an example. The challenge to shape a generation falls to you – what a privilege!

[1]   John 8:36
[2]   Proverbs 15:17
[3]   Hebrews 13:2
[4]   2 Timothy 1:5
[5]   Proverbs 24:30-34

CHAPTER 7

protecting The Bridge

W e have established that the second generation face a unique battle, one quite different from the *Battle for the Loins* faced by first generation believers. We have called it the *Battle for the Bridge* because their victory protects the line of continuity between the 'loins of origin' and the third and all future generations.

Learning to let go

Returning to the Bible narratives, Isaac was the second generation from Abraham. He was the bridge between Abraham and Jacob. Therefore, the relationship between Abraham and Isaac has much to teach us about the relationship between the first and second generations. One such incident is when they went to Mount Moriah together:

'*Some time later God tested Abraham. He said to him, "Abraham!"*

"Here I am," he replied. Then God said, Take your son, your only son, Isaac, whom you love, and go to the region of Moriah.

Sacrifice him there as a burnt offering on one of the mountains I will tell you about."

Early the next morning Abraham got ready and saddled his donkey. He took with him two of his servants and his son Isaac. When he had cut enough wood for the burnt offering, he set out for the place God had told him about. On the third day Abraham looked up and saw the place in the distance. He said to his servants, "Stay here with the donkey while I and the boy go over there. We will worship and then we will come back to you."

Abraham took the wood for the burnt offering and placed it on his son Isaac, and he himself carried the fire and the knife. As the two of them went on together, Isaac spoke up and said to his father Abraham, "Father?"

"Yes, my son?" Abraham replied.

"The fire and wood are here," Isaac said, "but where is the lamb for the burnt offering?"

Abraham answered, "God himself will provide the lamb for the burnt offering, my son." And the two of them went on together.

When they reached the place God had told him about, Abraham built an altar there and arranged the wood on it. He bound his son Isaac and laid him on the altar, on top of the wood.

Then he reached out his hand and took the knife to slay his son. But the angel of the Lord called out to him from heaven, "Abraham! Abraham!"

"Here I am," he replied.

"Do not lay a hand on the boy," he said. "Do not do anything to him. Now I know that you fear God, because you have not withheld from me your son, your only son."

Abraham looked up and there in a thicket he saw a ram caught by its horns. He went over and took the ram and sacrificed it as a burnt offering instead of his son. So Abraham called that place The Lord Will Provide. And to this day it is said, "On the *mountain of the Lord it will be provided."*

The angel of the Lord called to Abraham from heaven a second time and said, "I swear by myself, declares the Lord, that because you have done this and have not withheld your son, your only son, I will surely bless you and make your descendants as numerous as the stars in the sky and as the sand on the seashore. Your descendants will take possession of the cities of their enemies, and through your offspring all nations on earth will be blessed, because you have obeyed me." [1]

Here we see the first and the second generations separately putting God at the centre of their lives yet having to do it in a corporate experience. God was asking Abraham to sacrifice the second generation, the bridge to his generational future, and as such it parallels the sending of Jesus by God the Father to lay his life down for our sin. Abraham was surrendering the life of his only son. He didn't have others left at home and Isaac had been born to them late in life as a 'child of the promise' so no others were coming after him in the natural. I'm sure this was the last thing Abraham expected God to ask him to do considering the battle he'd fought to break free from his unbelieving family line.

Of course God never intended for Abraham to take the life of his son. God just wanted to know whether he would do it or not, it was a test of his obedience and faith. In the generational thinking context of our studies in this book, this incident was about Abraham being willing to let go of the second generation. It was about him being willing to let go of the control and protectiveness that he felt towards his child, something all first generation parents feel as they endeavour to protect the bridge their children represent to future generations.

I certainly felt this way about my girls. I tried to protect them because I didn't want them to miss God or to have to re-fight any of the battles I had faced. So I can only guess how Abraham would have felt in that he only had the one son to be the bridge to all that God had promised him. I'm sure that sometimes he just felt like wrapping him up in cotton wool!

As first generation believers, we must learn how to let the second generation go. Within this process there is a balance between abdicating our responsibility completely at one extreme and over protecting them at the other. We must be there for them but not smothering or controlling them inappropriately because that will have the opposite effect and potentially turn them against God. So, as Abraham was tested to find out whether or not he could let go of the second generation and allow them to find God for themselves, we too will be tested in this way.

Isaac's discovery

Through the Mount Moriah experience, Isaac learned some very important things. Firstly, he learned with some finality that his father Abraham would actually let him go. If ever he doubted it or felt a little smothered or over-controlled by his protective first generation parent, this shattered that illusion forever. There he was standing over him with a knife; it doesn't get more final than that!

Secondly, through the experience Isaac found God for himself. When you are laid on an altar with a fire about to be lit beneath you and a knife hovering over your heart, you are going to find something out about God in that moment. Isaac had to trust God just as much as Abraham. I would venture to say that in that moment Isaac truly learned to trust God for himself, for his own life and destiny.

Then both Abraham and Isaac looked and saw the ram in the thicket. Each were filled with gratitude as together they discovered that God does provide. God doesn't just provide for the first generation, he provides for each successive one as they put their full trust in him. In that life-changing moment God revealed himself and his purpose to Isaac, the second generation. We must always remember this as first generation believing parents. We had a life-changing encounter with God, he met us and broke us out of our godless natural family lines, he introduced himself to us with an impact that has sustained the momentum which has resulted in us raising a second generation of believers in our homes. But we must allow God to introduce himself to the second generation himself. They cannot live off our faith, beliefs, or encounters with God, they must have their own.

Glenda and I have faced these challenges together. We have had to let our girls go and allow them to find God for themselves. God has been good to Glenda and I, and the children have reaped all the benefits that go with being raised in a godly home as we have explained elsewhere in this book. But each of them individually had to discover that God is not just good to mum and dad, he is also good to them.

don't force it, model it

It grieves me when I see first generation parents forcing their children to attend church with them or putting undue pressure on them to be spiritual. Whatever you do, don't force your children to be in church so that you look good. I know it is tempting because if they aren't living like angels it can reflect badly on you, particularly if you are in leadership. So the temptation is to put up with them living like devils all week and then bribe or beg them to come to church with you and behave like angels on Sunday. And because children will to a certain extent do things to keep mum and dad happy, they comply. But it's not from their heart and it is actually doing more harm than good and hindering their ability to encounter God meaningfully for themselves.

Sadly, many second generation children don't follow in the faith of their parents because they forced God upon them. Don't force it, just be content to model the liberating, wonderful life that you have in Christ before them, and release them to discover God for themselves. In the releasing environment of a happy and healthy Christian home, God will introduce himself to them. Our greatest task as first generation parents is therefore to model a God that they will want to love and know. We must model a God who is fun, relevant and not religious or legalistic. It starts at home and then extends into our churches. We must do all we can to ensure that we model the truth about who God is and the wonderful place his House is. If we get this right, the second generation will thrive as they happily and voluntarily put down roots into the fertile soil of God's House right next to ours.

make god Irresistible

One potential difficulty that second generation children face is that they encounter the church long before they encounter God. They were raised in the church but if for whatever reason it was not a good experience for them, they will begin to dislike the church and start counting the days until they don't have to go anymore.

The fact is that God is much more attractive and easier to love than much of the church. Churches riddled with legalism and dead traditions are a complete turn off to every second-generation young person. So, as first generation believers we have a great responsibility to ensure that the churches we are taking our children to are filled with things that show them a God they can easily love and follow. The church must endeavour to make God irresistible to her second-generation children because ultimately it is their relationship with him that will sustain them.

I have observed that many second generation children simply follow in the footsteps of the faith of their parents but get confused by their church experience. They find it hard to love the church and mistake this to mean that they can't or don't love God. But often times the truth is that they haven't actually met God yet, they just had a bad church experience. In these situations, fearful parents then begin to pressure their children to be in church and a pattern of resentment and resistance sets in. Before long there is a breach not only between the child and the church but between them and their Christian parents. Many second generation children in this situation leave the church disillusioned and damaged, and are labelled as backslidden, but in actual fact they were never born again in the first place.

So, to all first generation parents I want to say, please don't try to make your teenagers go to church, especially if you know that it's dead, dull and boring.

Protecting the bridge generation starts at the source of the new line of faith and the church environment they are born into or develop in. Because the church was the context within which I learned God's ways, the church's view on things really mattered to me. So, if the church said a certain behaviour was good, I believed them and began to raise my children, the bridge generation, in line with it. Only now do I realise that right from the start the church was potentially hindering my second generation from embracing the God I loved by establishing a whole range of church practices which misrepresented God and turned my children off him. As parents we have a responsibility to model a God our children will want to love, and as churches we must do the same. In this way we protect the bridge generation and create a context within which they can win their personal *Battle for the Bridge*.

Do what works

For these reasons I have become very mindful about legalistically imposing any form or pattern of church life or spiritual lifestyle on my children. I have discovered that as long as we keep the bigger picture in mind, which is the successful transmission of a strong line of faith between the generations, it is OK to do what works in my own home.

For example, I remember a time when our girls were in Sunday school and they used to bring home worksheets every week for us to do with them before the next Sunday. Those worksheets became the bane of our lives. Every Saturday night before church we would frantically complete the worksheets to be handed in the next morning. Each week we vowed that we would do them earlier in the week next time but we never did. Of course they had to be done because I was the pastor and my children must be seen to be keeping the church rules! Gradually, those worksheets made me begin to dislike church, never mind the children. So, I banned them from my home. As I saw it, church had become an extension of school for my kids and I hated what it did to them. The children loved it! They began looking forward to going to church again for all the right reasons and that's the way we have tried to keep it. Church for our kids should be awesome, fun, happy, exciting. Today our Kids Church is fantastic and children from across the city can't wait to get there. Many of them are not even born again yet but they have no resistance to God or his people, courtesy of a church that models a God they can love.

The church's rules relating to acceptable models of Christian living can also creep into home life and do damage to the second generation very easily. The so-called 'right way' of doing things is affirmed to us and we can soon equate legalisms and methodologies with being the only way of doing a thing to please God. But usually it is not the case. Few of these things are fundamental and it is far more important that we outwork the spirit of scripture and live in the freedom of our salvation than it is we comply with patterns which should have been presented as a possible way of doing things rather than the only way.

I recall that when Glenda and I were first saved we received lots of 'advice' from people who knew we were first generation and didn't know how to raise our kids in a Christian way. So they tried to help us by telling us what the church taught about family life. We were told that we needed to pray with our children every night. So we did, whether they wanted us to or not. This led to some real disagreements as they grew! We were told that we should say Grace before every meal. So we did, which was quite a challenge in our hectic household. I was advised that we should have 'family altar' times, where I would gather the family and open the word of God with them in my role as priest of the home, sort of a family devotional time. I just knew that it would end in tears – world war three actually – so this never really happened. The problem was, they didn't tell us it wasn't working in their family either, they just imposed it on us as being normal Christian family life. We didn't know any different. So we just towed the line and sometimes did things that were not wise by pressurising our children. It wasn't smart and I quickly realised these things were not working for us, so we changed them.

My point is, do what works and don't let things which the second generation perceive to be church requirements ever get in the way of them meeting God for themselves in the context of a faith-filled home and church experience. We have got to build an empowering church where families are released to do whatever works for their children. All children are different. Some are stubborn, some are more gentle; some are eager to please, others are strongly independent. There is no one-size-fits-all when you have a house full of kids. Whatever works best for you is what you should do, otherwise you will potentially drive your children away from God, which is precisely what the devil wanted. Rather than protecting the bridge generation you have just become an accomplice in their demise.

First generation, we have got to be careful how we handle our children. School them from your walk with God more than from your church experience, especially if your church experience is weak, and keep it real with them.

Second generation, I believe one of your biggest challenges is choosing God for yourself. It's complicated for you because unlike your parents you met the church before you met God. So potentially the church becomes more real to you than God is. But it's harder to love the church than it is to love God. We don't want you trying to make the church God or ever believing that any struggle you have with the church is automatically a struggle with God. It's not.

Love and the loins

Before we leave this subject, I want to describe a situation I have witnessed a number of times over the years. It is very important in this context of protecting the bridge generation but actually has application at any time where two generations are seeking to preserve continuity of the godly line. It goes like this:

A second generation boy gets out of sorts with his parents because he is disillusioned with the church – as we have been describing above. He takes time out from church. In this period he meets the girl of his dreams. She is good looking, intelligent, everything his parents would have wanted in a girl except for one thing, she is an unbeliever. Undeterred by this he brings her home, fully expecting mum and dad to embrace his girlfriend with genuine warmth and enthusiasm. After all, he knows that they just want him to be happy – and he's never been happier than when he's with her. Mum and Dad don't dislike the girl but are seriously concerned that she is not a Christian and make their feelings known. Distraught by what he sees as their rejection he pronounces, 'I always knew that church was full of hypocrites. Didn't Jesus say we should love everybody? I always suspected there was no love in that church; you're all judgmental hypocrites'.

Some of you have been there as parents, some of you have been there as the young man in this example. To him I would say, you have created a bigger dilemma for your parents than you could imagine. To the parents I'd say, stand your ground because the stakes are bigger than this single relationship – the loins are at risk. I know it can be hard but as a parent you must explain to your child in this compromised relationship what the stakes are. Say something like, 'I love you and I want you to make it. But let me tell you why I can't receive that girl into our home; you are threatening my loins. That girl is threatening my lineage. My grandchildren are at stake if I receive her and encourage you to build a life with her, so I will not. She is unsaved and there is no love for God in her heart or life. Don't tell me that you are going to witness to her and get her saved because all you are a witness to at the moment is that you haven't got a strong enough faith to stay away from her and trust God with the situation'.

Sadly, nine times out of ten the unsaved person influences the Christian more than the other way round because they're second generation and they are so close to wanting a good sin that it goes the other way. But the fact is you must protect the bridge. Your child is asking you to welcome someone who may break the momentum of your spiritual genealogy.

Teenagers have a way of receiving advice like this as being from the parental 'drama queens' who they perceive to be out of touch with reality, whereas the converse is actually true. They may focus it into a personality issue, blame the church or God, but we must stand our ground as believing parents. Our very loins are being threatened. Our ancestry, our lineage, our line of faith to permanence is under threat. They are destroying the bridge they were meant to be and potentially forcing your grandchildren to re-fight the *Battle for the Loins* all over again.

Situations like these have led me to believe in arranged marriages, not in the conventional sense as practiced in many cultures in the world today, but following a biblical pattern. When Abraham was seeking a wife for Isaac, he went to extraordinary lengths to make sure she was from an appropriate lineage. He sent his closest servant to make the choice with clear instructions: He said, '*I want you to swear by the LORD, the God of heaven and the God of earth, that you will not get a wife for my son from the daughters of the Canaanites, among whom I am living, but will go to my country and my own relatives and get a wife for my son Isaac.*'[2] It was vitally important to Abraham that Isaac did not intermarry with the idol worshipping nations he was living amongst. Similarly, when God gave the law to Israel he forbade them from inter-marrying with the surrounding nations because it would threaten the loins of their heritage. Also, in the New Testament Paul instructed that if a Christian woman's husband dies, she is free to marry whoever she wishes as long as he '*belongs to the Lord*'.[3] That's an arranged marriage; God is arranging the circle of her choice. He doesn't choose the person for her but the circle inside which she is now free to choose. In this way the bridge between believing generations is protected.

To the second generation

Finally, to all second generation believers reading this, I want to say on behalf of first generation believers like myself: we salute you. We thank you for standing firm as the bridge you are in this generational linkage. We thank you for being strong. We thank you for waging the battle that's only yours to wage. Don't let us down. Don't let the devil bomb your bridge. Don't ruin what we fought and suffered for. Don't make our grandchildren have to fight it all over again. But stand firm and be a powerful bridge between the two generations you have been destined to keep a line of continuity between.

[1]   Genesis 22:1-19
[2]   Genesis 24:3-4
[3]   1 Corinthians 7:39

1987

'TRAIN A CHILD IN THE WAY SHE SHOULD GO,
AND WHEN SHE IS OLD SHE WILL NOT TURN FROM IT.'
PROVERBS 22.6

2003

'ONE GENERATION WILL COMMEND YOUR WORKS TO ANOTHER;
THEY WILL TELL OF YOUR MIGHTY ACTS'
PSALM 145.4

The Third Generation's Battle:

The Battle for permanence

CHAPTER 8

The Battle for permanence

'*G*od said to Moses, "*do not come any closer, take off your sandals, for the place you are standing on is holy ground*". *Then he said, "I am the God of your father, the God of Abraham, the God of Isaac and the God of Jacob". At this Moses hid his face because he was afraid to look at God.*'[1]

This is the first recorded time in scripture that God introduces himself as the God of three consecutive generations. Prior to this he had simply been 'the God of Abraham', then 'the God of Abraham and of Isaac' and now finally there are three generations. Between Jacob and Moses there had been many more generations but God didn't keep adding names on. After Jacob, God stopped. Once three consecutive generations had chosen to love and serve him, God stopped. This is significant.

I believe this pattern in scripture teaches us that if something can be established to a third generation, it seems to take on a permanence it didn't have in the first two. If a thing can survive with strength to a third generation, it develops a resilience that was not as pronounced in the first two generations. I think God is saying, 'if I can be the God of Abraham, that's good; if I can be the God of Abraham and Isaac, that's even better; but if I can be the God of Abraham, Isaac *and* Jacob, then this line of faith is established to three generations and it will now be safe forever'. And it has been.

Each generation in this progression has had a battle to fight as we have been discussing in this book. We have seen that the first generation must win the *Battle for the Loins*. This battle breaks them from their unbelieving background or family lines and establishes a brand new line of faith. The second generation must then fight the *Battle for the Bridge*. This unique struggle has as its aim the challenge of bridging the generations either side of them. If the second generation goes down and either rejects God or backslides from God, there is no bridge to connect the line of faith to the third generation, after which it is potentially going to be safer. The third generation's battle is then what I've called the *Battle for Permanence*.

As we have seen, each generation's battle is fought in a different arena. A significant part of the first generation's *Battle for the Loins* is fought in the supernatural arena. In the spiritual realm there are many things going on as the new believer breaks free from their godless past and establishes a strong new line of faith for their children to walk in. All hell breaks loose against the first person to break from Satan's grasp in a way it doesn't against the next few generations.

The second generation's *Battle for the Bridge* is fought in the arena of identity. They want to be distinct and not to just blend in with what their parents did. Second generation believers must find God for themselves from within a Christian family and church environment which has the potential to over protect them. Their battle is to find their true identity.

We now turn to the third generation's *Battle for Permanence* which is waged in the arena of inevitability. That's because after three generations, the power of individual choice becomes significantly overwhelmed by the generational force of inevitability. Strong willed people, which Jacob clearly was, resent just towing the family line and doing things because everybody else has. Indeed, that became his major struggle. The force of over sixty years of generational commitment to God in the family behind him made his commitment to God almost inescapable. So, the third generation's battle is played out in the arena of inevitability produced by the growing momentum of two generation's faith and their desire to make a personal, distinct choice - which though they have, they can feel it's a choice without options!

So, the point I am establishing here is that because God stopped introducing himself as the God of multiple generations at generation number three, it would appear that if anything is established for three generations, it takes on a permanence that it did not have in the first two. In fact after Jacob it became the faith of millions as his sons became the tribal heads of the nation of Israel. The permanence established in Jacob was sufficiently strong in its momentum to explode his faith into being the established faith of a nation.

Jacob's struggle

Jacob was the third generation of Abraham's line of faith and upon his life came the overwhelming momentum of his forefather's commitment to God. Having won his *Battle for the Loins* Abraham had raised Isaac to follow in his footsteps. Isaac won his *Battle for the Bridge* successfully holding both to the faith of Abraham and raising his son Jacob in a God centred home.

The Genesis account tells us that Jacob was born struggling and grasping for pre-eminence.[2] This was the beginning of what became a pattern in his troubled life. After years of living by his wits, scheming and plotting his way through life Jacob eventually hit rock bottom, he found himself alone with God and separated from his family and possessions. With his past rapidly catching up with him in the form of Esau and four hundred men, it was a make or break time for Jacob.

Throughout the night he wrestled with God over the issue of his identity.[3] Torn between his natural deceiving nature and the spiritual generational weight of his father's faith, it was to be a defining moment. Within his loins was the beginning of a nation waiting to be born into a home marked not by deceit and mixture but by the strength of permanence produced by decades of pilgrimage.

That night not only did Jacob's name change to Israel but so did his nature. He moved from being Jacob 'the deceiver' to Israel the one who 'prevails with God'. The line of faith had successfully run its course from Abraham, the loins of origin, over the bridge of Isaac to the tipping point of permanence in Jacob.

Momentum, inevitability and choice

I have described Jacob's battle as being with inevitability. However this does not remove the element of choice but it does highlight the fact that when we think and live generationally there is an incredible amount of momentum behind the third generation. That momentum is actually a gift to the third generation from the former two; it sweeps over them, urging them forward to perpetuate the line of faith. Momentum is the power of the movement the third generation are born into and it is an incredible gift and a positive asset if they can see it this way.

Momentum becomes so powerful that, like a boulder rolling down a hill, it flattens everything in its path. Eventually momentum gets so strong that it produces what I call 'the force of inevitability'.

Anything in its path will be squashed or removed; it's not an option. When it first started off, small things could stop it. But when it gets rolling, gathering weight and speed, it's not a case of 'will anything stop it?' Nothing will stop it. It is simply going to mow down everything in its path. The momentum results in everything resigning itself to the 'force of inevitability'. In human terms, the power of momentum becomes so forceful that it inevitably overwhelms the power of 'choice'. Therefore, the battle of the third generation is actually the struggle between 'the force of inevitability' and their freedom to choose.

The third generation of a family who are born into a God loving, God fearing, God serving family line like Jacob's, already have something approaching sixty years of momentum behind them. There's already the momentum of Abraham and Isaac, so by the time Jacob arrived the line of faith was so established and strong that God's ways were the normality of family life and values. It's as though the third generation are at the bottom of the hill and the stone began rolling fifty or sixty years ago from the top of the hill. By the time they're born in the path of that rock, it is travelling with such momentum that if they attempt to stand in its path and deny God or refuse to walk in the faith of their fathers, they will create more problems by their resistance than by going with the flow.

It doesn't mean that the third generation don't have a choice anymore. But it means that the weight and momentum of generational 'preference' is against them. And this is exactly what we're looking for in our individual families, churches, towns and cities.

If you think about it, this situation is exactly what we've got in our society today, only the other way around. We have the momentum of abuse, violence, abortion, racism, prostitution, drugs and violent crime. The momentum of these evils in our society is generationally speaking very old. It didn't start when we were born. For example the much reported race riots in my home city of Bradford were not caused by a new momentum, they were simply a new expression of an old momentum that has been rolling down the hill for many generations. Similarly, the 'boulder' of drug taking is now so strong in our cities that the 'force of inevitability' dictates that many thousands of babies born today will be either born with an addiction or almost inevitably dabble in drug taking of some kind by the time they are in their mid-teens.

As a result of these negative forces of momentum and inevitability, society has become paranoid and we tend to over protect our children in an effort to steer them away from all the bad influences out there. We flee the inner cities and relocate to the suburbs or countryside and let the inner cities implode as the 'boulders' crash down on them. Fear of the negative momentum in society gets into the fabric of our lives and infiltrates our souls. Fear swaggers around our towns and cities dominating the minds of people. It grips a nation's mind and paralyses a nation's heart.

stop!

And what are the people of God doing in the midst of all this? Some of them are also fleeing the mess of our towns and cities by retreating into church buildings that have become modern day monasteries. They retreat from the world and play church behind closed doors and stained glass windows while the world around them perishes under the momentum of evil in society. This is a tragedy; it is the abdication of our mandate and our generational responsibility.

But what can we do? The momentum of countless generations of evil set resolutely against God and his people is like the traffic in the fast lane of a motorway. To jump into the flow in an effort to reverse it would be inviting certain death, or so it seems. And the thought of doing that is so scary that many Christians say to themselves, 'I'm sure God understands and he won't mind if I just live my days out as a good person. I'll be in church, I'll tithe, I'll worship. But the negative generational momentum is so strong that our church would be completely messed up if we ever went into our city and said 'STOP' to the advance of evil.

Five years ago, that is exactly what our church did here in Bradford. We leaped out into the flow of generational momentum in the city and said, 'STOP!' We entered our schools and said 'STOP' to the force of inevitability that leads young people to try sniffing glue and solvents (Volatile Substance Abuse) and there have been no deaths from this in our city since that time. We jumped into the 'red light' district and have rescued a number of working girls from what they thought was the inevitable way they would have to live. We stood in the flow of homelessness, started reaching into the prisons, stepped into our universities and into some of our most deprived housing estates. We went in with our programmes, practical help and advice. We went with a smile and a big heart of love to help people believe they can have a better life. We jumped into the fast lane and effectively put our hand up to every demon and every evil that had dominated our city for generations and said 'STOP!'

Reversing the flow of momentum

Five years on and with the battle scars to prove it, people from around the world are now coming to see something of the difference we're making in our city. There is still a massive amount yet to do but this has taught us that it doesn't take long to begin to reverse the flow of traffic if you are serious about it. I believe that if we think in generational terms over the long haul, eventually the flow of momentum will reverse. Instead of the generational preference being 'against God,' there will be a generational preference 'for God.' Then, the only one standing in the motorway with his hand in the air saying 'STOP!' will be the devil, trying to stop the incredible momentum of the life of God's kingdom in our city. And we will not be swerving to miss him!

In a recent prayer meeting here in the church various ministry leaders were sharing something of their challenges and successes. As the evening continued it became clear that there were few places you can go in Bradford where you will not bump into someone or something to do with our church. We heard of the many thousands of primary and secondary school children who have enjoyed our lessons, assemblies, concerts and youth clubs; of the outreach on the university campus; a ministry reaching needy families with child support and life skills; the prison ministry; our ministry to the disabled and so it went on. It is increasingly hard to avoid this church if you live in this area, people just can't help bumping into us! And it is because the momentum is reversing; new lines of first, second and third generation believers are starting to influence their communities. The tide has turned!

Legacy of blessing and dominion

Adam and Eve's original mandate was to '*Be fruitful and increase in number; fill the earth and subdue it. Rule over the fish of the sea and the birds of the air and over every living creature that moves on the ground.*'[4] Dominion was God's plan right from the start. Sadly, our original parents failed and within a generation they had sent the world God created into the spiral of sin and godlessness that we are all naturally born into. But then came Jesus, the second and last Adam,[5] a new 'loin of origin' from which a new line of spiritual men and women would flow. In Christ we are born again, made alive spiritually and now form part of God's people on the earth. Our number one priority is to fulfil that original mandate, to fill the earth with people like Jesus and rule over his creation. Ruling means that we must proactively take control of situations that are contrary to God's word and ways. It means outworking the command of

Christ to love all people by going to them with the good news of a new life in Christ.[6] This is our mandate, it is the legacy of blessing we have for our world that is lost under the momentum of countless generations of God-haters.

Every time a first generation believer comes to Christ it removes a little from the enemy's generational momentum and adds it to Christ's. Then as it extends to a second, third and the generations beyond, the size of God's 'boulder' grows and the size of the enemy's diminishes. This is how the Kingdom of God grows, it gradually permeates and influences the whole of your community, town, city, nation and the world, as Jesus illustrated by the parable of the yeast.[7] As we begin to think and live in line with these generational concepts, fight the appropriate battles and dare to reverse the momentum of evil in our society, the prophecy of Daniel is moved towards fulfilment. He interpreted a dream in which a statue representing successive world kingdoms was shattered by a rock, which then grew and *'filled the whole earth'*.[8] The interpretation indicates that at the time of Christ, *'The God of heaven will set up a kingdom that will never be destroyed, nor will it be left to another people. It will crush all those kingdoms and bring them to an end, but it will itself endure forever. This is the meaning of the vision of the rock cut out of a mountain, but not by human hands.'*[9]

The Kingdom of God is that rock and it is destined to fill the earth with the knowledge of God. How will it happen? By doing exactly what I have described above, daring to believe you can make a difference, starting to work with these generational principles and contributing the legacy of blessing and dominion that is your birthright in Christ to the collective momentum of the 'boulder' which will one day fill the earth.

Breaking this down into very practical terms, the legacy of blessing you leave for the next generation in this flow of momentum is first and foremost your willingness to fight the battle appropriate to your generation. If it is for the *loins*, then fight it and win it. If it is for the *bridge* or *permanence*, do likewise. This in itself adds to the momentum. Then, do all that God has put in your heart to do in your lifetime. Set things up for the next generation, give them an 'assist' which helps them to put the ball in the net when it is their turn to be on the playing field. For me personally for example, it includes handing my spiritual children a debt free complex of buildings and resources from which to continue the work of reaching our city and the world. I want to hand them a legacy of the things that I fought for, for them. I want to hand them as best I can, buildings, vehicles, equipment, resources, projects, relationships and networks around the world. I want to hand them a legacy that I never had.

The devil's delay tactics

As I said above, we have done a lot in five years and proved that it is possible to start reversing the momentum in society. This is something the devil knows. He knows he is defeated, that '*greater is he that is in you than he that is in the world*'.[10] He believes and trembles! So he knows we can reverse the flow. His best tactic in each generation is therefore to try and stall the inevitable. If he can delay us, he robs us of some of our momentum and thereby survives a little longer.

I learned this five years ago when as a church we were effectively orphaned overnight. Everything we had known for the previous twenty-five years was removed by a decision to part company with the organisation we had been a part of. Looking back, I now realise I was the victim of a poor handover which cost me a few years of momentum. I should have had the baton in my hand probably five years sooner. So now one of my abiding frustrations is the thought that, if we have done this much in the last five years, where could we have been if we had been going at it for ten? This explains why as a church we have run so hard and believed God for such massive things – we have tried to live and work in a way that makes up for lost time! The devil robbed us of those years of momentum and we will never let it happen again because the future of all those in our loins are at stake.

The devil works smart. So don't look for a tail and horns, he's far more subtle than that. But the resistance, refusal and reluctance of any generation of spiritual fathers to hand over to their children, is one of the devil's greatest delay tactics for the growth and acceleration of the church. He aims to keep the spiritual children, who should have had their hands all over this thing by now, waiting and waiting and waiting, living in frustration, battling things they shouldn't have to battle.

Empower them now

Having seen this cunning ploy of the enemy, I have now determined that rather than make the same mistake, I'd rather be too trusting of the new generation. I have deliberately chosen to empower the young people in our church. I'd rather risk that they may let me down and learn from it, than delay empowering them and cause further delay to the momentum of God's life in this city through our church. It is for this reason that people have often said to me, 'all your staff are kids'. Sometimes it is because they are worried I have over empowered them too soon but I am not waiting until I'm an old man before I hand anything over! I'm empowering natural and spiritual children now. That's why one of the three core values we live by as a church is that we are 'people empowering'. It is now part of the DNA of our church.

This is not just about young people though. Some have become the new generation in our church, yet they are old in years. Indeed, some of the original young people did not 'cross over' with us into our new church five years ago. It's not about age it is about heart attitude, outlook and having a spirit that is free and eager to do something great for God in your generation. This is a generation of people who have a heart that's up for anything God wants to do. It's a church full of people with a Caleb spirit. He was described as a 'man of a different spirit' because he believed what God said in spite of the giants and walled cities that faced them as a nation. Likewise, the generation we are empowering are not fazed one bit by leaping into the generational flow of evil in our city and saying 'STOP!' It is what they were born for and the longer they have to do it, the greater the reversal will be in their lifetime.

It is time for God's people to wake up and play their part. Generational momentum removes the choice to such an extent that the babies born today in some areas of our city have no chance. By the time they're four or five they'll be using language that would make your hair curl! Before they reach the age of twelve some of them will be involved in crime. They will be regularly drinking alcohol, be exposed to sex, violence, immorality and even prostitution – the youngest prostitute we have ever come across was only thirteen years old. And the devil loves it. He looks at our towns and cities and says to himself 'I've had this city for generations, these kids have no chance and you Christians have no hope of changing it!' The church has believed that lie for generations. We've not believed in a God of dominion. We've not lived an overcoming, victorious life. Instead we've spent all our time counselling people who should have grown up a long time ago. We've been a church that has failed to think in generational terms and dared to believe we can really change the status quo of evil.

But what we've proved here at the Abundant Life Church in Bradford is that in a short space of time we can be big enough to stop all that. We can forget about 'us' and start thinking of 'them.' We can equip ourselves and the next generation for a multigenerational onslaught on the evil in society. We can start empowering people and passing the baton on. We can make a difference when we commit to the long haul of generational momentum and stop looking for the unreality of a 'quick fix' lifestyle both for ourselves and our communities.

Divine intervention

Many would say the only thing that can break the generational pattern of evil that is destroying society is a 'divine intervention.' I totally agree. However, by this I do not believe the intervention we are looking for is called 'revival' as some understand revival to be. God has always been committed to working through his devoted people. So, divine intervention looks a lot like you and me! It is called Paul, Charlotte, Stephen, Emma, Lara and whatever your name is as you read this today. You are the divine visitation your community is waiting for.

Jesus was the ultimate 'divine intervention' into the affairs of humanity. He came with a clear purpose which was, '*to destroy the devil's work*'[11] which is our mandate too. How did he do it?

'*God anointed Jesus of Nazareth with the Holy Spirit and power, and he went around doing good and healing all who were under the power of the devil, because God was with him.*'[12] And that's the way we have to do it too. We must take our God-filled selves out into the community and start doing good to all people. That is divine intervention.

Jesus came and gave a massive push to the 'boulder' that represents the generational advance of his kingdom in the world. This momentum is now two thousand years old, but because the church hasn't lived in accordance with the generational principles we have been discussing in this book, we don't actually have two thousand years of momentum behind us. Just imagine if we had! The devil on the other hand does have two thousand years of momentum behind him. Evil has continued from generation to generation all through that period and in some generations has had some massive boosts to its momentum. But things are changing. The church is waking from her slumber and realising that the power we have in Christ is far greater than the devil's. So much so that within a few short years we can make a massive difference. Compound this forward and you can see that within a few generations our towns, cities and nations can be transformed into communities where God and his church once again play a central part in the lives of people.

This is our goal. From it we must not flinch. Let each generation fight their battle thoroughly and pass the baton on to the next with ever increasing momentum until, *the whole earth is filled with his glory.*[13]

[1]   Exodus 3:5-6
[2]   Genesis 25:26
[3]   Genesis 32:9-30
[4]   Genesis 1:28
[5]   1 Corinthians 15:45
[6]   Matthew 28:19-20
[7]   Matthew 13:33
[8]   Daniel 2:35
[9]   Daniel 2:44
[10] 1 John 4:4 KJV
[11] 1 John 3:8
[12] Acts 10:38
[13] Psalm 72:19

CHAPTER 9

In closing

Ministering these truths and writing this book has changed my life. It has shaped the way I build the church, do ministry, empower people and raised my faith to a whole new level. God can fill the earth with an obedient people who think in generational terms and outwork these principles.

All I do now has longevity within it. I am building for permanence. While I still believe in 'seizing the day' I now take hold of it not for the short-term pleasure or gain it brings but for the long-term benefits it contains. In every life I reach today are thousands of others. The battle truly is for the loins of our communities.

If you were to die tomorrow, would all you had done in your Christian life die with you? If so, you are not building in a way that recognises and works with these principles of generational momentum. Everything you do should have a life that extends well beyond your own. When your plans are bigger than just your present life, there is a legacy developing that will live on in the generational momentum to which you contributed your life, strength and abilities.

Live full, die empty

The idea is that you live a full life but die empty. How sad if when you died, there were still things locked up in your bones that should have been passed on to the next generation. There they lie in your grave with you.

In the spring of 2000 I preached a message here in my home church called, 'Live Full, Die Empty'. It became a defining principle for our lives and ministry. We read that, '*Elisha died and was buried. Now Moabite raiders used to enter the country every spring. Once while some Israelites were burying a man, suddenly they saw a band of raiders; so they threw the man's body into Elisha's tomb. When the body touched Elisha's bones, the man came to life and stood up on his feet.*'[1] It would seem that years after he had died, locked up in Elisha's bones was a lost legacy of power and anointing. Somehow, in Elisha's human remains there was still a deposit of incredible power. What was that power doing locked up in his bones? I believe the reason is that Elisha died before he could get empty because it is possible for a person to die before they have fully discharged what God gave them to pass on in this life.

The destination of all our fullness is emptiness. As he has done since the beginning, the Holy Spirit can still be found hovering on the borders of emptiness, longing to get involved in filling it with God's life, order and rule.[2] God is drawn to emptiness not fullness. If we want to keep God involved in our lives and churches then we must keep finding empty vessels for him to fill. In the story of the widow's oil, God only stopped pouring when the widow ran out of emptiness. As soon as she could find no more empty vessels, God stopped pouring.[3]

It is clear that throughout his life, and especially in his last days, Elisha tried desperately to pass on his power and anointing. Remember, he had double Elijah's anointing and that was a great deal to give away. He tried to establish a legacy through his servant Gehazi who he sent to perform a miracle of resurrection on the Shunamite's son. But God would not work through Gehazi because his heart was not right.[4] Towards the end of his life and now on his deathbed, we again see Elisha desperately trying to empty himself of his remaining legacy of power and anointing.[5] This time he attempts to pour it into a spiritually dull king, Jehoash. Elisha instructed him to enact a prophetic sign of his victory over the king of Aram by striking arrows on the ground. But Jehoash was so spiritually dull that he missed the point of striking the arrows on the ground and stopped after doing it three times.[6] This aroused Elisha's anger who finally realised that he was about to die with much of his power still locked up inside him.

Elisha's power could not go with him to heaven because what God gives us for this life cannot be kept and used in the next life. In heaven, no sick need healing, no poor need feeding, no lost need reaching and no visions need financing. All of this activity can only be done on earth. What we don't use here will stay locked up in our bones like a lost legacy of power with nowhere to go

This story has made me more determined than ever to die empty. I want to die with nowhere left to go, nothing left to do, no one left to help, no sermons left to preach and no money left in the bank except maybe an inheritance for my children. I want to die with dignity, like King David who died at a good old age, having enjoyed long life, wealth and honour.[7]

The apostle Paul died empty too. Towards the end of his life he wrote to the young man Timothy: '*For I am already being poured out like a drink offering, and the time has come for my departure. I have fought the good fight, I have finished the race, I have kept the faith. Now there is in store for me the crown of righteousness, which the Lord, the righteous Judge, will award to me on that day – and not only to me, but also to all who have longed for his appearing.*'[8]

It was as if Paul felt that just before he died, God was squeezing every last drop of wisdom, revelation and impartation out of him into young Timothy and the churches. Paul was determined to die empty. Paul did not believe in dying with the 'secret recipe.' He believed in passing everything on that he possibly could through both his letters which endure to this day and the lives of the next generation of believers to whom he was passing the baton.

However, the ultimate 'dying empty' scene is depicted by Jesus on the cross. In his final agonising moments of life, it was as if he was holding on for one more opportunity to pour himself out. With his dying breath he snatched the thief on the cross next to him from hell. He looked deeply into the eyes of the centurion in charge of his crucifixion and said '*Father forgive them, they know not what they do.*' This was the centurion's moment of revelation that Jesus was the Messiah.[9]

Jesus, still determined to die completely empty, looked down on his now widowed mother standing there with sorrow in her eyes and held tightly by the Apostle John. Realising the incredible pain she was going through he said to her "'*Dear woman, here is your son' and to John he said 'Here is your mother.*'"[10] From that time on the Bible says John took her into his own home. Having done everything that could have possibly needed doing, the scripture tells us that Jesus said the three most powerful words ever spoken in history, '*It is finished.*' He did not say, 'I am finished' but 'it' meaning his work, purpose, and divine commission. He then bowed his head and gave up his spirit. His head did not drop, he bowed it. Like an actor leaving the stage for the last time, Jesus majestically bowed out and entered the grave empty. Nothing was left undone this side of the grave.

I am therefore determined that there will be nothing left in my bones when I die. I am committed to living full but dying empty and I pray with all my heart that you will too.

If yours is the *Battle for the Loins* as a first generation believer, wage it with tenacity and courage because you are the 'loins of origin' for all who follow. Make a strong start.

If yours is the second generation's *Battle for the Bridge*, protect it with a passion. Ensure both ends remain strongly in tact so that the legacy from your spiritual fathers travels through to your own children.

And if you are fighting the *Battle for Permanence* today, I pray that as you find God for yourself, you will happily add your strength to the already fast-flowing generational momentum of faith you were privileged to be born into.

[1]   2 Kings 13:20-21
[2]   Genesis 1:2
[3]   2 Kings 4:1-7
[4]   2 Kings 4:29-31
[5]   2 Kings 13:14
[6]   2 Kings 13:18-19
[7]   1 Chronicles 29:28
[8]   2 Timothy 4:6-8
[9]   Matthew 27:54
[10] John 19:26

2004

OUR FIRST GRANDCHILD HOPE CHERISH

THIRD GENERATION

acknowledgements

❖ To our four daughters: **Charlotte, Bethan, Ruth and Esther**. I love you and am proud of you all. You are all a credit to God and your Mum and I. Thank you for being great kids. Thank you for being a strong bridge to permanence.

❖ To **Charlotte** my oldest, my firstborn. On the day that you were born the angels got together and decided to make a dream come true for your Dad's ministry. You became the best helper, assistant, PA and armour bearer any pastor could ever wish for. Now, to see you emerging in your own distinct anointing and commissioning is my greatest joy. What a formidable team we are. We are like a huge first and second generation combination punch. Our relationship is special and what I really love about it is that no one really understands that 'specialness' except you and me. I love you Charlotte.

❖ To **Steve Gambill, Mark Stevens** and **Mitchell James**, my three sons-in-law. Thank you for being the awesome men of God you are. I am proud of you. You enrich our lives and you strengthen our bridge.

❖ To **Stephen Matthew**, my co-pastor and friend for over twenty years. Thank you, Steve, for your priceless help with this book and for sharing something of your story in it. Thank you for standing with me as we fought and won the Battle for the Loins of this church. May we live to see our spiritual third generation bring permanence to the work of our hands.

❖ To **Hope Cherish**, my first grandchild. You light up my life. You are so smart it's breathtaking; your power and ability to imitate anything you see is genius. Hope, God's House is in your house so your life will doubly flourish. May all the force of inevitability overwhelm your life. I love you Hope.

Full details of other resources by
Paul Scanlon are available from:

Abundant Life Church
Wapping Road, Bradford
West Yorkshire BD3 0EQ

Tel: +44 (0)1274 307233
Fax: +44 (0)1274 740698
Email: admin@alm.org.uk

For a copy of our free quarterly magazine 'Voice to the Nations'
please contact us as above.

Visit our online store at www.alm.org.uk

Browse the full range of preaching, teaching, training, music
and worship resources available from Abundant Life Ministries

Other book titles available from
Abundant Life Resources:

It's Not Over 'Till The Barren Woman Sings
by Paul Scanlon

Crossing Over
by Paul Scanlon

Consumer or Consumed?
by Charlotte Scanlon-Gambill